THE TECH SET

Ellyssa Kroski, Series Editor

D0730920

User Experience (UX) Design for Libraries

Aaron Schmidt and Amanda Etches

ALA TechSource

An imprint of the American Library Association

Chicago   2012

Printed in the United States of America

Library of Congress Cataloging-in-Publication Data
Schmidt, Aaron, 1978–
    User experience (UX) design for libraries / Aaron Schmidt, Amanda Etches.
      p. cm. — (The tech set ; #18)
    Includes bibliographical references and index.
    ISBN 978-1-55570-781-1 (alk. paper)
    1. Library Web sites—Design. 2. User-centered system design. I. Etches, Amanda, 1975– II. Title.

Z674.75.W67S43 2012
006.701'9—dc23

                    2012007200

⊗ This paper meets the requirements of ANSI/NISO Z39.48-1992 (Permanence of Paper).

*This book is dedicated to everyone who is working hard
to create usable and interesting libraries.*

CONTENTS

Don't miss this book's companion website!
Turn the page for details.

**THE TECH SET® Volumes 11–20 is more than just the book
you're holding!**

These 10 titles, along with the 10 titles that preceded them, in THE TECH SET® series feature three components:

1. This book
2. Companion web content that provides more details on the topic and keeps you current
3. Author podcasts that will extend your knowledge and give you insight into the author's experience

The companion webpages and podcasts can be found at:

www.alatechsource.org/techset/

On the website, you'll go far beyond the printed pages you're holding and:

- ► Access author updates that are packed with new advice and recommended resources
- ► Use the website comments section to interact, ask questions, and share advice with the authors and your LIS peers
- ► Hear these pros in screencasts, podcasts, and other videos providing great instruction on getting the most out of the latest library technologies

For more information on THE TECH SET® series and the individual titles, visit **www.neal-schuman.com/techset-11-to-20**.

FOREWORD

Creating usable websites involves much more than knowledge of HTML. Effective website design is a user-driven process that anticipates the needs of actual site visitors by consulting them throughout the course of development. *User Experience (UX) Design for Libraries* is a complete how-to handbook that instructs readers about how they can utilize user-supplied data to inform their information architecture decisions by conducting open and closed card sort studies and how to stage live usability testing sessions and focus groups. This outstanding primer by UX experts Aaron Schmidt and Amanda Etches guides the reader through how to create heuristic evaluations, the ins and outs of persona development, and developing a content strategy. Readers will walk away knowing how to build a first-rate website in partnership with their library patrons.

The ten new TECH SET volumes are designed to be even more cutting-edge than the original ten. After the first ten were published and we received such positive feedback from librarians who were using the books to implement technology in their libraries as well as train their staff, it seemed that there would be a need for another TECH SET. And I wanted this next set of books to be even more forward-looking and tackle today's hottest technologies, trends, and practices to help libraries stay on the forefront of technology innovation. Librarians have ceased sitting on the sidelines and have become technology leaders in their own right. This series was created to offer guidance and inspiration to all those aspiring to be library technology leaders themselves.

I originally envisioned a series of books that would offer accessible, practical information that would teach librarians not only how to use new technologies as individuals but also how to plan and implement particular types of library services using them. And when THE TECH SET won the ALA's Greenwood Publishing Group Award for the Best

Book in Library Literature, it seemed that we had achieved our goal of becoming the go-to resource for libraries wanting hands-on technology primers. For these new ten books, I thought it was important to incorporate reader feedback by adding two new chapters to each volume that would better facilitate learning how to put these new technologies into practice in libraries. The new chapter called "Social Mechanics" discusses strategies for gaining buy-in and support from organizational stakeholders, and the additional "Developing Trends" chapter looks ahead to future directions of these technologies. These new chapters round out the books that discuss the entire life cycle of these tech initiatives, including everything from what it takes to plan, strategize, implement, market, and measure the success of these projects.

While each book covers the A–Zs of the technology being discussed, the hands-on "Implementation" chapters, chock-full of detailed project instructions, account for the largest portions of the books. These chapters start off with a basic "recipe" for how to effectively use the technology in a library and then build on that foundation to offer more and more advanced project ideas. Because these books are designed to appeal to readers of all levels of expertise, both the novice and advanced technologist will find something useful in these chapters, as the proposed projects and initiatives run the gamut from the basic how to create a Foursquare campaign for your library to how to build an iPhone application. Similarly, the new Drupal webmaster will benefit from the instructions for how to configure a basic library website, while the advanced web services librarian may be interested in the instructions for powering a dynamic library website in the cloud using Amazon's EC2 service.

Both *Library Journal* Movers & Shakers, Aaron Schmidt and Amanda Etches have been writing and speaking about usability and libraries for many years. These two authorities on user experience design teamed up to craft an exceptional book full of insightful nuggets of wisdom for achieving a top-notch website based on user feedback. If you're seeking to learn all that's involved with creating usable websites, *User Experience (UX) Design for Libraries* is the book for you.

Ellyssa Kroski
Manager of Information Systems
New York Law Institute
http://www.ellyssakroski.com/
http://oedb.org/blogs/ilibrarian/
ellyssakroski@yahoo.com

Ellyssa Kroski is the Manager of Information Systems at the New York Law Institute as well as a writer, educator, and international conference speaker. In 2011, she won the ALA's Greenwood Publishing Group Award for the Best Book in Library Literature for THE TECH SET, the ten-book technology series that she created and edited. She's also the author of *Web 2.0 for Librarians and Information Professionals*, a well-reviewed book on web technologies and libraries. She speaks at several conferences a year, mainly about new tech trends, digital strategy, and libraries. She is an adjunct faculty member at Pratt Institute and blogs at iLibrarian.

PREFACE

By picking up *User Experience (UX) Design for Libraries* you have already acknowledged the importance of improving your library's website. We couldn't be happier! As user experience (UX) designers, we firmly believe that making all your web design and functionality decisions with the user as your primary focus will result in a better design, a more intuitive interface, and a more enjoyable experience for your users. *User Experience (UX) Design for Libraries* shows you how to get there by providing hands-on, practical steps, tips, advice, and best practices for using UX design principles, practices, and tools to engage your users online and build the best, most user-centered web presence for your library.

▶ ORGANIZATION AND AUDIENCE

This concise guide in nine chapters covers everything you need to jump in to using UX practices to improve your library's website. In Chapter 1, we introduce you to the field of UX design, why it's important, and what we think library websites should do. We also deal with some central tenets that guide our thinking on library website design. In Chapter 2, we get into the types of solutions available, including hardware and software options for UX designers. In this chapter, we also introduce the UX design techniques that we will explore in greater detail in Chapter 5. Chapter 3 deals with planning for web projects, starting with the important issue of whether you should redesign your website at all (as opposed to iteratively designing it), as well as how to perform a needs assessment of your website. Chapter 4 is all about social mechanics—you will learn about the roles and responsibilities of a web team and how to get buy-in for your web projects from everyone from library administration to your systems department, the rest of your staff, and, most importantly, your community.

Chapter 5 is about implementation. This is where we delve into the details about how to conduct a usability test, how to perform a card sort, how to develop personas to inform your web design decisions, how to perform a heuristic evaluation of your website, and how to write a content strategy. In Chapter 6, we get into marketing, starting with some ideas around how thinking about your library website as a "virtual branch" can help you with your marketing efforts. This chapter also covers traditional marketing opportunities, search engine optimization, social media marketing, how to communicate and market your website redesign (which is arguably one of the biggest web projects that you'll undertake!), some ideas to promote transparency in your web development activities, and, finally, how to market internally.

In Chapter 7, we discuss some best practices that we have observed in library web design and highlight some of our favorite library websites that are doing things specifically well in the areas of search, navigation, authenticity, orientation, the mobile web, visual design, community engagement, and web writing. Chapter 8 gets into the difficult topic of usability and user experience metrics, and we discuss the utility of tools such as website analytics, A/B tests, surveys, and five-second tests. Chapter 9 rounds out the discussion with some commentary on what we see as developing trends in library website design, specifically around discovery and access to library resources and the issues around developing websites that are optimized for mobile devices. In the final section, Recommended Reading, we leave you with an annotated list of some of our favorite print and web resources for UX design.

We'll be the first to acknowledge that there are literally hundreds of books out there on UX design. So, we are both thrilled and humbled that you chose *User Experience (UX) Design for Libraries*. We think you made the right decision because our experience as librarians *and* UX designers gives us a unique perspective on the needs of libraries, librarians, and, most important, library users. We've tried to distill this perspective in a way that can help you go out there and build better experiences for *your* library's users. We hope you find it useful.

▶1

INTRODUCTION

▶ WHAT IS USER EXPERIENCE (UX) FOR THE WEB AND WHY IS IT IMPORTANT?

User experience for the web is all about how users feel when interacting with a website or interface. As you might imagine, web UX is a small subset of a larger discipline that deals with how users feel about interacting with *anything*: a system, product, service, or space. For the purposes of this book, when we talk about UX, we're really referring to web UX, which, as a discipline, is a coming together of the fields of information architecture, interaction design, interface design, and usability.

However, at the heart of it, UX is so much more. If you have ever experienced sheer delight when using a website that is simple, easy, understands what you are trying to accomplish, and helps you get there, then you know that a good user experience is also about how a well-designed website makes you *feel* (important, delighted, competent, and any number of other positive adjectives). At the same time, if you've had the misfortune of using a website that is confusing, one that puts up roadblocks at every turn and doesn't help you accomplish what you set out to, you know that a bad user experience is also about how a poorly designed website makes you feel (frustrated, annoyed, incompetent, and many other negative adjectives)!

▶ 1

This is exactly why UX matters. It's not difficult to come up with a clean, streamlined information architecture for your site; it's also fairly easy to work through all the interactions on a site to create a functional interaction design; and, as you will see, usability testing your site isn't rocket science—it takes some time and planning, but it's a fairly straightforward pursuit. But all of these practices rolled up together is what ensures that positive experience for your users.

▶ WHY SHOULD LIBRARIES CARE ABOUT UX?

You've already made it to Chapter 1, so we're guessing you don't need a lot of convincing about why libraries should care about UX. However, we feel it's important to reiterate that the principles of good web UX should matter a great deal to libraries, because we are already fighting an uphill battle when it comes to our users' attention. Content and information are no longer scarce commodities that require the mediation of the library—thanks to the web, both are plentiful, which has changed the value proposition of libraries. As we continue to retool to respond to the changes in the information marketplace and meet the needs of our users, it is more imperative than ever that we are attentive to our web presences, providing online experiences that are simple, intuitive, and delightful.

▶ THE LARGER SCOPE OF UX AND HOW IT RELATES TO WEB UX

As we mentioned previously, the website designs and interfaces you expose your users to are only part of the whole user experience picture. Ideally, all of your library's touch points—the places where your users come into contact with your library—will be aligned and well designed. This means that creating a holistic and positive user experience includes designing great print materials, signs, customer service, facilities, reference work flows, programs, collections, and services. This might seem daunting. It is indeed a lot of work and sometimes difficult. But it is crucial for the success of your library.

The experience you try to facilitate through your website is an important component of the total user experience you provide. It is often the first touch point with which people come into contact. Patrons use it frequently as the gateway to your catalog and other online resources and services. It is also a challenging piece of the UX puzzle. While you likely have different physical spaces for different types of library users, creating distinct digital spaces isn't necessarily desirable. However, with adequate user research you can create a website that will meet the needs of your most important audiences.

▶ WHAT A LIBRARY WEBSITE SHOULD DO

Most website behavior is task oriented: people have an information need or need to accomplish something and they use the web as a tool to meet that need. There are a few websites that people browse for fun and entertainment, but your library's website probably isn't one of them.

Library websites should differ as much as the communities they serve differ. Conversely, library websites will share many characteristics because of the similarities of people everywhere. Libraries' responses to these similarities should make up the basic functionality of every library website—things like library hours, locations, services, loan period information and catalog searching should be included. Getting these basic things right—something that few libraries do—is the first step to creating interesting and thriving library websites. It doesn't make sense to build on a shaky foundation, but many libraries do because it is relatively easy. As additional functionality gets tacked on, websites quickly become complicated, and information that patrons want becomes increasingly difficult to find. This book encourages you to get the basics right first before you consider taking your website to the next level.

▶ THE CATALOG PROBLEM

Your website is not as important as your catalog. This is a fact. We've asked many nonlibrarians about what they do on library websites, and the usual response is "Place reserves on books." This is subtly different from how we think of our websites and catalogs (i.e., as distinct things). So, either our users see the two as the same thing, or they ignore our websites and just use our catalogs. Looking at website analytics suggests the latter.

The primacy of the catalog is understandable and unfortunate. It is understandable because people want to accomplish things by using websites. In the case of libraries, the number one critical task is access to content. For public libraries this means books, movies, and music. For academic libraries, add in journal articles. It is unfortunate, because we have very little control over the visual and interaction design of our catalogs. This is worth repeating: we have very little control over the look and behavior of the number one thing people want to do on our websites. The solution to this problem isn't within the scope of this book, but it is a problem that we want to acknowledge. Having well-designed library websites will get us only so far. To provide the ability to find library items, some libraries will still subject their users to an interface that is not only different from the rest of their website but also one that is poor. This lack of control over the catalog is the number one problem for library websites.

▶ CENTRAL TENETS

The techniques in this book will help you create a user-centered website. Here are some things we believe about library websites that inform our designs and will help you create the better websites.

Less Is Less (and That's a Good Thing)

Your goal is to make your library's site as small as it can be while still meeting the needs of your users. This will result in patrons finding stuff with greater ease and less ongoing maintenance for your web team.

Patrons Don't Read Library Websites, They Scan Them

Nothing against your library website, really. People don't do much reading on the web period. Instead, people hope to learn bits of knowledge or accomplish tasks. Knowing this fact should impact the way we write for library websites. Information should be presented in easy-to-skim chunks.

Good UX for One Is Good UX for All

Accessibility is an extremely important issue for websites. So much so that web accessibility is often legally mandated for public organizations (depending on what country/state/province you're in), and, because most libraries are public organizations, compliance with web accessibility guidelines is a pressing matter for most of us. While this book does not specifically aim to make your website compliant with whatever accessibility legislation you operate under, we believe that adhering to web accessibility standards is not a limitation but an opportunity. Much like universal design is all about improving design and usability to the benefit of everyone, making your website accessible will improve the experience of your site for *all* your users, not just the ones who use adaptive technology for their browsing needs.

A Library Website Isn't a Portal to the Web

With near ubiquitous and constant web connectivity via computers and mobile devices, the entire notion of a starting place on the web is a bit dated. Even if it wasn't, patrons wouldn't start their web experiences on your library's website. They don't visit your library's site for links to their e-mail or to find out the weather or to find search engines. If your site has them, remove these extraneous bits.

Library Websites Are for Library Users, Not Librarians

Sometimes portions of library websites are designed for librarians to use on the job. When librarians are accustomed to using the library website daily it can be difficult to redesign the site for patrons. If you face resistance when removing librarian-centered content from your website, put the content in question on your staff intranet. If you don't already have one, consider creating one. You can adapt the techniques in this book to design a website for library staff, too.

When in Doubt, Leave It Out

You should be able to strongly articulate reasons for including every single thing that's on your library's site. If you're not sure why something is on your site and can't find a reason, remove it. The same thing goes for content that is considered "nice to have" on the site. Everything on the site should be essential. If it is not essential, it shouldn't be there.

►2

TYPES OF SOLUTIONS AVAILABLE

- ► **Consider the Hardware**
- ► **Review the Software**
- ► **Incorporate New Techniques**
- ► **Determine Your Scope**

Excellent user experiences don't just happen. We need to create them. Like all things that are made, creating a user experience requires tools. Here are some suggestions for assembling a collection of tools to help you create the best website you can.

►CONSIDER THE HARDWARE

Paper, Pencils, and Markers

Get in the habit of sketching all your ideas, both big and small. Not only will this help you keep track of ideas, but sketching is also an important part of the iterative design process. Giving yourself the freedom to explore half-baked ideas let's you quickly evaluate, get feedback, and learn from them. When sketching, start off using fat markers so you don't get bogged down with detail. Refine as ideas solidify.

Computers and Peripherals

Use whatever operating system you're most comfortable with to create your website, but consider having both a Windows and a Mac environment as well as various mobile devices with which to test your site.

If you plan on recording usability tests, you might want to consider the following hardware peripherals:

> ► **A microphone to capture audio.** Almost any will do, even the Logitech USB Desktop Microphone for under $20. Likewise, you'll need speakers on the other end for observers.
> ► **A webcam to capture your testers' reactions.** Again, any webcam will do the trick, so don't worry about spending too much on a premium camera.
> ► **A video camera.** For some usability tests, you might want to set up a video camera behind your testers so you can capture their screen activity and movements. Getting a camera that you can easily set up on a tripod is best for such tests.

► REVIEW THE SOFTWARE

Usability Testing Software

In Chapter 5, we delve into details about types of usability tests, when to do which, and what tools you need to complete various types of tests. As you will see, most types of usability tests can be done using low and no tech, but if you would like to do things like record screen activity and user input, here are some software options to consider.

Morae
http://www.techsmith.com/morae.asp

Morae is the Cadillac of usability testing software to capture audio, video, and screen activity during usability tests (when you use it with all the necessary peripherals like a microphone and a webcam). Morae also produces full-featured reports that make it easy to analyze test results across testers. At $1,500, Windows only.

Silverback
http://silverbackapp.com/

Silverback is the lighter, cheaper alternative to Morae that does most of what Morae does and is probably more than sufficient for 95 percent of the usability testing you will do at your library. At $69.95, OS X only.

Infomaki
http://sourceforge.net/projects/infomaki/

Based on the popular Fivesecondtest software (http://fivesecondtest .com/), Infomaki is a free, open source usability testing application that allows you to remotely test interface designs via the web.

Usabilla
http://usabilla.com/

This hosted usability testing website provides one free usability test and relatively cheap options beyond the first test.

Userfly
http://userfly.com/

Userfly is another online, hosted usability testing site that captures video of tests and hosts them for clients. Userfly has both free and subscription options.

Wireframes and Mockups

An essential step in the web design process, creating wireframes and mockups of your designs will help you visualize the end result at every step of the design process and even allow you to test your designs on paper while shaping the final product. We are fans of keeping it simple when it comes to creating wireframes and mockups (a pen and grid-lined paper are a wireframer's best friend!), but there are a couple of software and online tools that can get you higher-tech results, if that's what you're looking for.

OmniGraffle
http://www.omnigroup.com/products/omnigraffle

This software is good for mocking up page layouts and making wireframes. At $99.95, OS X only.

Mockingbird
https://gomockingbird.com/

This online tool allows you to create your wireframes on the web and link multiple wireframes together. Free and subscription options.

Mocksup
http://mocksup.com/

Another free/subscription online mock-up tool, Mocksup allows you to upload your designs to the site and use the built-in tools to test those designs with users.

Lovely Charts
http://lovelycharts.com/

A simple and elegant online drawing tool, Lovely Charts is free and provides all the elements to create your wireframes and mockups in an online environment and then download your output locally.

Image Creation and Editing

The heavy hitters from Adobe like Illustrator and Photoshop might have a place in your toolbox. If you're familiar with them, great. If not, that's okay, too. You don't necessarily need to learn complex image software to build better online experiences. Here are some alternatives worth considering.

Acorn
http://flyingmeat.com/acorn

Dubbed "the image editor for humans," Acorn has plenty of functionality wrapped in a usable interface. There's a free trial, and the paid version is $49.99. OS X only.

Pixelmator
http://www.pixelmator.com/

A bit more expensive than Acorn at $59.99, it is also robust and easy to use. OS X only.

GIMP
http://www.gimp.org/

This open source image editor is free and runs on Windows and OS X.

Skitch
http://skitch.com/

This user-friendly screen capture tool lets you easily annotate and share images. There are free and premium versions.

Browsers

Test your site in a number of different browsers across multiple platforms. Download multiple versions of Safari, Firefox, and Internet Explorer, and make sure your site renders well in all of them. There are also websites to help with cross-browser testing such as BrowserLab (https://browserlab.adobe.com/en-us/index.html) and Litmus (http://litmus.com/alkaline/).

Screencasting

You might want to occasionally record the computer screen while you're usability testing. Other times you'll want to display the usability test while people observe remotely. Camtasia (http://techsmith.com/camtasia/) is a good choice, and it costs $299. We like ScreenFlow 2 (http://www.telestream.net/screen-flow/overview.htm) as well, and it is less expensive at $99. Another option worth checking out for quick screencasts is Jing (http://www.techsmith.com/jing/), which comes in free and premium versions.

For a more in-depth treatment of screencasting, see *Screencasting for Libraries* by Greg R. Notess (THE TECH SET #17).

Project Management

Creating a great user experience takes good organization. We've found Basecamp (http://basecamphq.com/), a web-based tool, useful.

Card Sorting

Card sorts are such quick and simple tests to perform, it's hard to imagine needing software to do them! However, there could be occasions when your card sorters cannot come to the library to perform the tests, so these applications allow you to perform card sorts online. See "Perform a Card Sort" in Chapter 5 (pp. 40–45) for more detailed information.

OptimalSort
http://www.optimalworkshop.com/optimalsort.htm

OptimalSort provides a simple, online interface to set up both open and closed card sorting exercises that you can invite testers to perform. A one-year license is $990.

WebSort.net
http://websort.net/

Another online interface for closed and open card sorts, WebSort.net also provides impressive reports with the results of every sorting exercise. It costs from $149 to $2,499, depending on the number of tests and testers.

▶ INCORPORATE NEW TECHNIQUES

The following solutions aren't pieces of software. They're user research techniques that are essential for creating excellent websites.

Usability Testing

Usability testing is an essential tool for finding what's not working on your website. See "Conduct a Usability Test" in Chapter 5 (pp. 31–40) for details.

Card Sorting

This can help you with organizing and labeling your website. See "Perform a Card Sort" in Chapter 5 (pp. 40–45) for details.

Personas

A persona document represents library users and the process of learning about them. See "Create Personas" in Chapter 5 (pp. 45–56) for details.

Content Audits

Knowing what content you have helps you create a website that has content that your users really want. See "Conducting a Content Audit" in Chapter 5 (pp. 61–65) for details.

Surveys

Surveys can be useful for gathering people's opinions. Because we should be more concerned with how people actually behave rather than their opinions or how they say they will behave, they're our least favorite user research technique. Consider using a tool like SurveyMonkey, sparingly, to inquire about people's task completion rate and overall level of satisfaction on your website.

► DETERMINE YOUR SCOPE

Appropriately scoping your website project is an extremely effective technique that you should use to improve the user experience of your website.

The first thing to do when scoping your website is to determine who your potential audiences are and what content would meet their needs. See "Create Personas" in Chapter 5 (pp. 45–56) for more about this. Next examine the amount of staff resources you have to devote to your website. Every aspect of the site should be considered: content, design, and development.

Look at the needs of your audiences, your library's capabilities, and your current website. Read the list of important content for your site sequentially and ask your web team "Given the absolute must haves for our site (e.g., hours of operation, location, and contact information) and our current resources, can we do the best job possible if we add this content or feature?" As soon as the answer becomes "No" it's time to stop. You've scoped your site.

Don't be afraid of having a small website, because smaller websites are better websites. They're easier to build and maintain, and they're easier for patrons to navigate. It is better to have usable and relevant content for fewer people than it is to have a lousy site for everyone. When you scope your site it will likely require getting rid of some features and content. Use a Content Audit (also detailed in Chapter 5) to help you decide what to cut.

The technique of appropriately scoping a project can be applied to nearly every UX endeavor. In general, aim to do fewer things better.

▶3

PLANNING

Any project worth undertaking is worth planning. Planning your website design or redesign is no different—putting in a bit of legwork before embarking on such a project will allow you to properly scope the project, plan your timelines and milestones, figure out the project work flow before beginning the work, and avoid the dreaded "feature creep." In this chapter, we walk through the steps and issues to keep in mind as you plan for such a project.

▶DECIDE WHETHER AN ITERATIVE DESIGN OR A REDESIGN IS BEST

Many of you probably picked up this book because you are embarking on a large-scale website redesign and you'd like to have a road map for how to manage the project and end up with a more user-focused site. Well, here comes the bad news: we don't think you should redesign your website at all. No matter how much of a disaster it is.

Right now there is probably a little (or loud) voice going off inside your head proclaiming, "but our website is so awful that we really need to blow it up and start over!" While the temptation is great to kill your existing website with fire (especially if it hasn't received adequate attention in recent months/years), we'd like you to step back, take a deep breath, and consider a few issues first.

▶ DO WHAT THE PROS DO

Think about five of the most popular, functionally rich websites on the web: Facebook, Amazon, Google, Apple, and Netflix. Now think about the last time each of these sites went through a major redesign. Still thinking? That's because none of them has ever blown up its designs and started over. They have chosen instead to slowly evolve.

Imagine getting in your car and finding that the steering wheel has moved to the passenger side. And to the backseat. And that the accelerator and brake pedals are reversed. You'd be confused, right? And the car would probably be difficult to operate. Website redesign projects, even if they result in a better website, are likely to confuse the people who have been using your site the most. All the bellyaching that happens whenever Facebook makes a small interface or functionality change is one good example of this. Humans are creatures of habit, and, as web users, we adapt to designs, even the most jarring ones, by figuring out our own patterns and workarounds to accomplish what we need to. Forcing users to change their habits and adapt to an entirely new design is unfriendly at best and agonizing at worst.

▶ UNDERSTAND THE REDESIGN WOES

Most website redesign projects take a long time—usually at least a year for your average library website. We have been involved with enough major website redesign projects to know that the lack of visible progress often lowers staff morale and forces users to have to interact with a stagnant website for a large amount of time. Add to that the divided efforts involved with working on a redesign project while still maintaining an old website, and you can see one very good reason why we are not fans of large redesign projects.

Additionally, website redesigns are often fraught with internal politics and homepage land claims. If you have ever administered a website for a large organization, you already know that everyone wants a piece of the homepage pie. Everyone also has opinions about colors, layout, whitespace, images, font, and just about every other design element on a webpage. Our advice for the simplest way to avoid these unnecessary arguments is to avoid putting your homepage/design up for grabs in the first place. Which means forget about redesigning.

▶ CONSIDER THE ALTERNATIVE: ITERATIVE DESIGN

The alternative to a major website redesign is not status quo (as much as it might seem like we're trying to talk you into learning to love your existing, poorly designed website). Instead, the alternative we recommend is to *iteratively design* your website. Once again, those popular websites we mentioned earlier (Facebook, Amazon, Google, etc.) are worth analyzing for how they manage their design changes. Rather than redesigning their sites every couple of years, sites like Facebook and Amazon have chosen to make small, iterative changes to their designs. That's because small, iterative changes spread out the cognitive load required to learn new things on a site. Additionally, iterative design changes are kinder on staff, too, and can actually boost staff morale with small, frequent, demonstrable victories. Similarly, your users will also benefit from a constantly improving site.

▶ DON'T TAKE THE EASY WAY OUT

Even though there's a pile of reasons not to, many organizations redesign anyway. Why? Simply put: it's a lot easier to redesign your website than it is to put into place the website governance structure and work flow required to iteratively design and constantly improve your site. The truth is, libraries can often avoid any significant organizational change by redesigning instead of consistently designing. It's often easier to form a special redesign team than it is to examine the current working culture and create a fluid and constantly collaborative environment. This is a bit of an organizational crutch, and projects can suffer because of it. It is a much more difficult—and much more valuable—task to create an environment that makes people comfortable working together on projects that are never truly done.

▶ EASE THE TRANSITION

There are some things you can do to make moving from a linear to iterative development process easier.

> ▶ **Give it a trial run.** Instead of forcing everyone into a new way of working, propose trying to fix a few things on the website and then debrief about the process.
> ▶ **Set small goals.** Don't aim to have a totally new website in six months. Improve one page, feature, or navigation element per month. Stick to these deadlines and build on these successes.

> ► **Don't launch the first solution you come up with.** Design many different options, run them past your team, and run a few small tests on the best options.
> ► **Instead of talking about preferences, elevate the discussion and get people talking about what's best for users.** Require that some initial testing take place before someone can suggest a change to something on the site.
> ► **Embrace the fact that no solution will be perfect and can always be improved upon later.** On the other hand, don't use this as an excuse to launch crummy designs.

► PERFORM A NEEDS ASSESSMENT

In today's web-driven information world, it is probably fair to say that every library needs a web presence. But needing a web presence alone is not a sufficient reason to build, design, or redesign a website. The very first step on the road to web development is to figure out the following:

> ► Library needs
> ► User needs
> ► Organizational capacity

In the user experience literature, these three needs are usually visualized as a triangle, with each of the three sides of the triangle represented by the three needs (see Figure 3.1). Each of the three sides of the triangle are equally important, because if you build a website that doesn't meet all needs as well as organizational capacity, your website cannot possibly be a success. The trick, of course, is to flesh out all three sides of the triangle *and* balance them accordingly. Before we get into the balancing act (which is probably the most difficult part of the process), let's take a closer look at how to determine each of the three needs.

Determining Library Needs

When determining the organizational needs for the library website, it helps to ask yourself a few questions:

> ► What are the mission, vision, and purpose of the website?
> ► What are the areas of strategic importance to the library (e.g., collections, services)?
> ► What does the library need to accomplish via the website (e.g., enhance outreach, attract more library users)?

▶ Figure 3.1: The Triangle of Needs

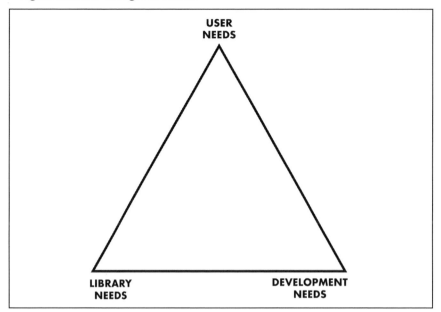

▶ What metrics will help the library prove that it is meeting its goals via the website (e.g., page hits, reduced bounce rates—see Chapter 8 for more on website metrics)?

A good way to gather this information is to start with the library's mission and vision statements and planning documents. Chances are, these documents outline all the organizational goals that are most important to the library. Additionally, think about creating a staff survey prior to embarking on the website project, asking the questions listed earlier, as well as other related questions. Another method is to

Mission and Vision Statements

If you've read any management/business literature, you know that operating without a mission and vision statement is like sailing a rudderless ship. We're not here to fix everything that's wrong with your library, but we do think it's important to situate any major website changes within the context of the organization's values and goals. So if you don't already have mission and vision statements, why not take the opportunity now to create them? As you're crafting these statements, keep in mind that your library mission should succinctly communicate what, how, and for whom you do what you do, and your vision is all about what you're striving for in the future.

gather library staff together for a few brainstorming exercises to help uncover the organizational needs and goals. If you can tap into existing strategic planning exercises to gather this information, you will be able to avoid duplicating efforts.

Determining User Needs

The best way to determine the needs of your users is to ask them. Luckily, there are a number of simple and effective ways to engage your users to help you determine what they need from the library website.

Surveys

Quite possibly the simplest, most cost-effective way to get feedback from your users about their needs and expectations for the library website is to create a short, online survey. When developing your survey, keep in mind that it is best to ask users about their habits and goals rather than what they would like from the website in terms of content and functionality. Gathering information on their habits and goals will require a bit of overhead on your part, as you will have to take your survey data and make some assumptions and guesses about your users' needs based on their habits. However, you will find this process to be a great deal more effective than, for example, presenting them with possible website functionality and content and asking what they would use.

Focus Groups

Gathering a variety of users together for a guided discussion about their use of the library website is another way to gather useful feedback on their goals and needs. Here, too, make sure you steer clear of questions about website content and functionality and focus the discussion on what users need to accomplish on the library website. Keep the group small—any more than eight participants and you will find that some members of the focus group might become intimidated and choose not to participate in the discussion as much as they might like to.

User Interviews

Performing one-on-one interviews with users is the most time-consuming, and therefore costliest, way to gain feedback from your users on their needs. It is also our favorite method. Here are some reasons why:

> ▶ One-on-one conversations get to the heart of user habits and behaviors better than any survey or focus group can.
> ▶ The conversational mode allows the interviewer to get clarification on things that come up during the interview.
> ▶ The organic, fluid nature of a one-on-one conversation allows the interviewer to zero in on the important issues and steer the conversation away from less important stuff.

For more on conducting user interviews, see Chapter 5 (pp. 46–47).

Card Sorting

A very specific type of needs assessment, a card sort is an exercise that can uncover user needs and biases by asking users to sort pieces of website content into categories that make sense to them. For a complete overview of the benefits of card sorts and how to conduct them, refer to Chapter 5 (pp. 40–45).

Determining Organizational Capacity

Organizational capacity is all about the resources you have within your organization to put toward meeting both library needs and user needs. To determine the organizational capacity side of the needs triangle, you should think about resources such as technology, personnel, and branding. Ask yourself the following questions:

Technology

> ▶ What server(s) will you use?
> ▶ Do you need a content management system?
> ▶ Will you use open source solutions, or will you purchase/license the technology resources you need (server administration, content management system, database applications, etc.)?
> ▶ Will you host your website internally, or will you pay an external hosting company to house your website?

Personnel

> ▶ Do you have the staff to build/maintain your website internally?
> ▶ Will you contract out the building/maintenance of your website to an external company/organization?

Branding

> ▶ Does your library already have a well-developed brand and marketing plan that you have to work within?

▶ Are your branding decisions governed by an external group/organization (e.g., some public libraries have to conform to city/county branding guidelines, and some academic libraries are forced to work within campus branding guidelines)?

Balancing Library Needs, User Needs, and Organizational Capacity

By now you're probably realizing that the needs assessment portion of your web project is a bit of a balancing act. As we mentioned previously, the three needs are usually visualized as the three sides of a triangle, which inherently indicates that all three needs should be equally weighted. While it is important to pay close attention to all three, in reality, it is often impossible to give them equal weighting. The refrain we hear most often is that while you can design for user needs as much as possible (while respecting organizational capacity), sometimes organizational needs (e.g., senior management) trump user needs and you are forced to make changes—sometimes at the very last minute before your new website is launched! Here are some ways to minimize this possibility:

▶ When determining the library needs portion of the process, get senior management involved as much as possible and get them to *sign off* on the results of the library needs assessment.

▶ Try to enlist a member of senior management as the project sponsor.

▶ Keep your library's strategic plan in mind always—if you ignore it, you're almost certain to miss the key goals that are important to your library and to senior management in particular. And if you take your cue from the strategic plan, all other staff and management requests for the website that don't fall in line with the library's goals can be more easily argued away.

Ultimately, if you build/design/redesign your library website with a specific purpose in mind, and if that purpose accounts for library and user needs and is respectful of your organization's capacity, you will be well on your way to making all your stakeholders happy.

▶4

SOCIAL MECHANICS

- ▶ Organize a Web Team
- ▶ Get Buy-In
- ▶ Balance Consultation and Progress

As you embark on any web-related project, you probably gaze long-ingly into the distance at the anticipated launch date as the desired end goal, after which everything will fall into place and life will be easy again. Alas, once your project launches, it moves from the project management phase into the operational phase, and it's usually in the operational phase when things go awry. Managing a project from idea to launch is sometimes the easiest part—it's how to take that project and build the necessary governance and support around it to keep it running and succeeding that's so much harder! In this chapter, we'll cover the mechanics of organizing a web team, managing a website, and getting buy-in from your stakeholders so that your project doesn't fizzle after launch, but continues to thrive and succeed.

▶ORGANIZE A WEB TEAM

Whether you're a web team of one or you're working with a team of people that spans different parts of your organization, it is important to think about all of the different roles required to create and maintain a website that provides an excellent user experience. The following list makes explicit who is responsible for what when it comes to keeping the website running.

Spelling it out helps everyone know how what they're working on fits into the larger picture and who to turn to with specific questions. You can also use it as an aspirational tool to help you plan what sorts of positions you should have and how your organization is structured.

Keep in mind that the roles listed do not need to function on a one-to-one ratio; in some cases one person will play many roles, and in other cases one role can be filled by a team of people. Also remember that these roles do not necessarily reflect job titles—the roles can be filled by anyone in the organization, from librarians to programmers to graphic designers—and will depend on individual skills and interests.

Administration

- ► The Web Administrator orchestrates the whole operation and is ultimately responsible for all aspects of the website.
- ► The Web Administrator is usually the primary point of contact with library stakeholders as well as with the Development Lead, Content Lead, Design Lead, and anyone else as needed.

Design

- ► The Design Lead identifies areas for improvement, plans user research, and suggests design improvements. This person works with library stakeholders, the Web Administrator, Development Lead, Content Lead, and anyone else as needed.
- ► The User Researcher plans user research, performs usability tests and card sorts, and conducts user interviews. This role works with the Web Administrator, Design Lead, Development Lead, and Content Lead.
- ► The Website Designer is responsible for the visual and interaction design of the website and usually works with library stakeholders, the Web Administrator, Design Lead, Development Lead, and Content Lead.

Development

- ► The Development Lead makes sure the site is online and the servers are healthy. The person in this role works with library stakeholders, the Web Administrator, and Design Lead.
- ► The Website Developer implements the website plan and is responsible for any programming that the website requires. This role works with the Web Administrator and the Website Designer.

Content

(These roles are further fleshed out in "Content Roles" in Chapter 5, pp. 68–71.)

- ▶ Content Requesters are those members of your organization who suggest additional content, removal of content, and edits for the website.
- ▶ Content Creators write web copy and produce all the content for the site, including creating multimedia and digital objects (PDFs, videos, etc.).
- ▶ Content Editors are your site's fact checkers and proofreaders. They are the folks who edit your site content in accordance with a preestablished style guide.
- ▶ Content Approvers do the final check and sign-off before content gets published.
- ▶ Content Publishers do just that—press the button to make content go live once it has received the nod from all the other content roles listed.
- ▶ Web Content Leads oversee the entire content process, establish the style guide and all other guidelines, and are responsible for auditing and assessing web content on an ongoing basis.

If you look closely you'll notice that, unlike other web team members, design team members work with everyone else on the web team. Why? Because design is important. It is crucial to providing an excellent user experience, and the design team needs an intimate understanding of all parts of the website process. This isn't to say that the design team should have complete control of every decision. Everyone must work together to find a balance of user needs, library needs, and development capabilities. This can be illustrated using the equilateral triangle shown in Figure 3.1 (see p. 19). If any one side of this arrangement is weighted too heavily, the process and site will suffer. For instance, library stakeholders and designers can suggest unrealistic ideas that the Development team isn't able to support. Or the Development team can drag its feet on implementing a user-centered design.

These teams shouldn't be housed in discreet silos. The more interaction between the teams the better. New ideas and updates shouldn't have to wait for a monthly meeting. With this flexible and fluid arrangement, your web team will have an easier time practicing the iterative design process we described in Chapter 3.

▶ GET BUY-IN

Getting stakeholder buy-in for your web projects makes them run smoothly. Stakeholders are those members both within and outside of your organization who have a stake in the success of your website. Therefore, it's important to think about how to get buy-in from stakeholders such as library administration, your systems department, other staff members, as well as your community (users, faculty, board members, etc.).

Library Administration

It is probably safe to assume that no project, web or otherwise, can really succeed without the blessing and support of library administration. When it comes to web projects in particular, support and buy-in from senior administrators is crucially important, given that the website is one of those resources that impacts every staff member in the organization. For example, to complete a successful website redesign, you will likely need a great deal of staff time, a budget (for servers, systems, testing, marketing, etc.), and approval to even embark on the project. If you are in a position to have to sell a web project to library administration, here are some ideas for how to get their buy-in:

► Talk to administration early and often. When you're starting your web project, draw up a project charter and ask a senior member of administration to be the "project sponsor" and sign off on the charter. Your project sponsor is your readymade project advocate and will help further your cause with the rest of administration.

► Send administration brief but frequent project updates. There is no such thing as too much communication.

► Involve as many members of administration as possible in the user research and usability testing phases of the projects (as observers). There is no better way for them to get a really good sense of the impact the website has on users than to have them watch a usability test or two. You will have them beating the UX drum on your behalf in no time!

Systems

While you might need administration's blessing to embark on web projects, support from your systems office is even more crucial! Chances are, your systems or IT department does all your server maintenance and is probably also responsible for any programming or scripting that has to be done to make your website function. This means having the systems staff on your side is priority #1! In some organizations, the website itself might also be managed by someone in the systems department, but in others the website might fall under the purview of a staff member in public services or marketing. In the latter scenario, a close, collegial relationship is even more important to the success of every web project, from the biggest redesign to the smallest maintenance issue. Here are some strategies we've used for getting buy-in from systems staff:

- ▶ Invite a member of the systems department to be on your web project team. Getting systems in on the game early is the key to keeping them engaged and preventing any last-minute systems roadblocks.
- ▶ We mentioned earlier that involving administration in the user research/testing phases of the project will help them see the value in the project; well, the same is true of the systems staff. This is especially the case when the project you're working on is particularly user centered.

Staff

We've already talked about getting administration and systems on board, but we also think it's important not to stop just there when it comes to library staff. Every member of your organization can and should be an advocate for your web projects, so consider taking the time to involve as many staff members as possible in your web projects to get buy-in early and maintain their engagement with the website. Here are some ideas for getting buy-in from all staff:

- ▶ Engage your content providers in the project process as much as possible. These are the folks who will own the content on the site once the project has been launched, so it's crucial for them to be involved from the earliest stages. This will help them take ownership of and be accountable for the content eventually.
- ▶ One of the best ways to engage staff is to start by simply providing them with plenty of opportunities to provide input into the process and the final product. In Chapter 5, we recommend starting a project blog to be transparent about the process and engage your audiences; that project blog could also be used to engage staff and elicit feedback as the project progresses.

Community

As important as it is to have website advocates inside your building, it is equally (if not more) important to get buy-in from your community, whether that's users or faculty members or members of your library board. An engaged user community can be a scary thing, because it usually means that you will hear from them regarding every little change you make to your website, good or bad (and, let's face it, people complain louder than they commend), but when the alternative to vocal engagement is despondent apathy, we usually recommend vocal engagement! These are some ideas for how to engage your community in your web projects and get buy-in:

▶ Invite a member (or two) of your community to join the project team. Having a community presence on the team does wonders for goodwill, but it also goes a long way to getting buy-in from everyone from users to staff members. When they know that users have not only provided input into the final product but have also been part of the project process, they will be more willing to accept and endorse the decisions that the project team has made.

▶ If your library already has an advisory committee (made up of community members or students) or a Friends group, use both groups as resources or consultants to the project team (you don't want the project team to be too large, so use them as occasional participants). Share project briefs and updates with both groups, and give them plenty of opportunities to provide input into the final product.

▶BALANCE CONSULTATION AND PROGRESS

We're not oblivious to the possibility that all this consultation and involvement from everyone from staff to community members could grind your project to a halt. How do you balance the goals of the project with the need to run as collaborative a project as possible? We wish there was a simple answer to that question. The plain truth is this: it's a really hard thing to do! But we don't think it's impossible. The best, more transparent, and consultative web projects we've been a part of have succeeded because the following ideas were at the fore-front of all their planning and implementation:

▶ **It's all about the user.** Keep the user at the heart of your decisions at all times. For example, if the project team reaches a stalemate about a particular decision, ask your users to break the stalemate; if staff input on certain design aspects of the site (from color to layout to placement) provide conflicting results, run a quick

A/B test with users to help you make the decision. Deferring to usability test results and user behavior/preferences will help you defend your decisions a lot easier and will remove the temptation to fall back on personal opinions.

A/B Testing

Tired of listening to people spout off their opinions about how a page should look? Bring some science to the table with A/B testing. These tests allow you to assess the performance of different versions of a webpage. The software serves different versions of a webpage to different website visitors and tracks their behaviors, so you can see the outcomes of their viewing each type of page. The tests work best when there's a direct behavior, such as clicking through to another page or downloading a file, that you want to measure. For instance, you could measure which of two library card sign-up forms leads to more successful completions.

Try Google Website Optimizer (http://www.google.com/websiteoptimizer) or Visual Website Optimizer (http://visualwebsiteoptimizer.com/) to get started.

▶ **Stick to the plan.** The project plan, that is. We've mentioned before that every web project should start with a project charter, one that includes detailed notes on scope, milestones, and timelines. Without a well-defined project scope, your project runs the risk of being infected with "scope creep," that notorious inevitability where the project parameters continually get pushed out and new features get added. Without solid milestones and timelines, your project could easily go off the rails and never reach launch date! However, when you have a project plan in place (that has been signed off on by the entire project team, as well as library administration), you are in a much better position to keep the project on track and deny any additional feature requests or scope changes at a later date, once the project has launched. With a good project plan in place, you will find yourself saying, "that is beyond the scope of this project" or "that will have to happen in another phase of the project," and that is just fine. In fact, it might be the number one contributing factor to the success of your web project!

Thinking of users and sticking to your plan won't provide a magic bullet, but they will help you keep your web project on track while still engaging your staff and community and getting their buy-in along the way.

►5

IMPLEMENTATION

- ► Conduct a Usability Test
- ► Perform a Card Sort
- ► Create Personas
- ► Perform a Heuristic Evaluation of Your Website
- ► Create a Content Strategy
- ► Arrange Content Work Flow

Now that we've discussed the types of solutions available and how to plan for UX, let's get to the heart of the matter and talk about some specific UX techniques and practices to help you improve your library's website.

►CONDUCT A USABILITY TEST

To improve your website you need to watch people interact with it. Observing an average user attempt to accomplish tasks on your website will provide you with insights you can gather in no other way. This is what usability testing is all about—the simple act of observing people interact with your website or interface will provide you with more user-focused insight than all the books about user-centered design combined.

Decide What to Test

You've decided that you want to improve your website by conducting a usability test. Excellent. Now you need to figure out what it is you want to test because you can't test your entire site right away.

Determine Critical Tasks

It makes sense that you should first test things on your site that are critical to your users. Ideally you'd use personas (see the section on personas later in this chapter) to help you determine the most important tasks for the main audience types of your site. But if you haven't (yet) developed personas, there are other ways to think about critical tasks.

Ask Some Library Users

This is quick and easy. All you have to do is walk around your library, or anywhere in your community really, and after introducing yourself ask people, "What do you do on the library's website?" Challenge yourself to ask up to 30 people and record their responses. Group all similar responses, and rank them according to frequency. You now have a list of critical tasks that you should consider testing first.

Brainstorm with Staff

This is a less desirable option, especially because going straight to library users is so simple. But if, for some reason, you can't find any library users, you can ask library staff what they think are the critical tasks patrons need to perform on your website. Ask them explicitly to think like a library user. You can also ask them for their perspective while reinforcing the fact that it is most important to first improve parts of the site that are critical for patrons. They might suggest testing things that they've received negative feedback about. They might suggest testing things that are their pet projects. Whatever the case, don't squash any enthusiasm about testing. Let them know that the library will provide a clear plan for what's going to be tested, when, and why.

Look at Web Statistics

Look at some cold, hard numbers to see where people are spending most of their time on the site. Again, this isn't as reliable as actually asking people what they do on a site. It is difficult to assess why people spend time on a particular page by looking at web analytics results. They could remain on a page or section of a website because they're confused and trying to find what they want; they could be enjoying rich content; or they could have simply walked away from the computer. After you use a combination of these techniques to come to an agreement about what tasks to test first, you'll need to sort out how you'll present these tasks to your testers.

Develop Scenarios

Now that you know what tasks you will investigate first, it's time to turn the process into something that's easy for your testers to understand and also doesn't give them any hints. Let's say you want to test how you label subscription databases on your website and the search interface, too. The following instruction would be quite leading:

> "Search a library database for an article about exercise."

If the term "database" appears on the website people are likely to figure out where to click and your test won't really test anything. Instead, give people some context and a story. A more effective prompt for this test follows.

> "You want to run a marathon and want to know how to train for it. Find the latest information in a magazine about training for a marathon."

This is a concrete task that testers can conceive of doing but at the same time it doesn't give them too much information. While it might seem like overkill, make sure these scenarios are clear by testing them with someone other than the person who wrote it. This will ensure that when test day comes your testers will know what you want them to do.

After you've crafted your scenarios make sure to print them so they can be clearly read by your testers after you've read it out loud. It is also a good idea to provide a copy of the scenarios to your testers so they can follow along while you give them the scenario and ask them to perform the tasks.

Set Tester Parameters

Once you've decided what needs testing and you know how you're going to present the tasks to people, decide how many and what kind of test subjects you want.

Five Is Enough

One thing that makes usability testing easy and relatively inexpensive is that you don't need to conduct many tests to find the majority of problems with completing a task. It is a commonly held belief among usability professionals that five participants will uncover 85 percent of usability problems on any given website, so aiming for five testers to begin with is usually enough.

Any Nonlibrarians Will Do

Because you don't need to conduct many tests, you don't need to recruit an exorbitant number of people to be your testers. The even better news is that, as long as they're not librarians, it pretty much doesn't matter who they are. Unless you have easy access to a specific demographic that matches the audience for something you're testing, don't worry about finding an exact match.

One factor that you should consider is how much web experience people have. An absolute beginner might not have the technical facility to use a mouse or might not understand web jargon (like "back button" or "search box") that you might use during the test. Keep this in mind as you recruit your testers.

Now Recruit Testers

As mentioned previously, recruiting test subjects can be as simple as walking around your library and asking library users for a few minutes of their time. You could also set up a table in a local mall, community center, student center (if you're on a college campus), athletic facility, or just about anywhere where you're likely to be able to attract walk-by traffic. Once you've grabbed the attention of a possible tester, you probably want to take a minute to ask a couple of "screener" questions to determine if he or she is a good candidate for the test. The screener questions will depend entirely on what you want to test. For example, if you'd like to start by determining basic computer competence, you might ask him/her how much time he/she spends using a computer on an average day and if he/she knows how to browse the web.

It is important to note that the recruitment method you use will depend almost entirely on who you want as testers. If you're looking to tap into your existing user base (which you will want to do most of the time), recruiting users in the library or via a call for testers on your website would be your best bet. The assumption here is that if they are in the library or on your library website, it's safe to assume they are existing users. If, on the other hand, you'd like to get feedback from nonusers, the community recruitment method (that is recruiting passersby in a location other than the library) would serve you well.

Offer Compensation

Providing some sort of compensation to your testers for their time is a good idea. Your library might not be allowed to pay people for their time or might already have another mechanism for doing so, but if not, consider providing gift cards as an alternative or using your Friends of the Library group as a go-between. Also, depending on your audience, you might be able to hook your testers with very simple rewards like a printing card for the library, amnesty on their library fines, or a free pizza lunch (all valuable rewards to cash-strapped college students, for example!).

Follow Usability Testing Best Practices

To get the most value out of your time (and your testers' time), here are a few commonsense practices to keep in mind and follow when conducting your tests.

Set Up the Test Room

If you are conducting your tests in person (rather than remotely), there are a few things to think about and do to make sure the physical environment is conducive to testing. You will want to start by making sure that the space is neat, clutter free, and free of distractions so your tester can concentrate on the task at hand. If you're recording the audio of the session (discussed later), make sure the microphone is close at hand and test it ahead of time for input volume. As a facilitator, it's a good idea to sit beside your testers so you can pay attention to their keyboard and mouse movements, and you will also get a better sense of their reactions and frustrations when completing the assigned tasks.

Write Scripts

Just like you've written a scenario that will provide consistency across all of the tests you conduct, you should also write a script to read during the tests. Giving testers even slightly different instructions could affect the outcomes of the tests. Scripts ensure that all testers receive the same directions and take the guesswork out of conducting the test. A script will allow you to concentrate on observing the tester and making him or her feel comfortable rather than forcing you to think about what you're going to say. These are some script essentials:

- ▶ Introduce yourself, and clearly outline your role during the test.
- ▶ Be clear about the purpose of the test.
- ▶ Provide testers with an outline of what they will be doing and how long it will take.
- ▶ Ensure that your testers know that they are not the ones being tested. This is probably the most crucial part of your script, so be clear about the fact that there are no right or wrong answers, actions, or ways to complete the assigned tasks.

► Reiterate to the tester that watching him or her perform the tasks you present will help you and your organization gain a better understanding of how people use the website/interface (whatever it is you're testing) so you can improve upon them accordingly.

Understand the Facilitator's Role

The single most important role for the test facilitator is to listen. We can almost guarantee that, as the test facilitator, you will be tempted to prompt your tester, react to what they're doing, and/or offer "helpful" guidance while they attempt to complete the tasks. This is especially the case if you, as the facilitator, have been involved with the development of the site/interface being tested! It is absolutely crucial to resist that temptation, however, because the goal of the test is to get an accurate indication of the usability of the site/interface, so if the facilitator becomes too involved in providing feedback or direction, the validity of the test results will be compromised. So, remember to just sit back and listen!

Depending on the test, you might also want to encourage your testers to verbalize what they are doing at every step of the test. This is crucial if you're audio-recording the test, but it is also extremely helpful if the facilitator is taking notes during the test. If, for example, you are testing your website, it will be helpful to know why the tester uses the back button or site search. Chances are your testers will pause at various points during the test, so having them verbalize their actions will provide insight into why they pause where (to read the content, to orient themselves, etc.).

Know What to Record

All test recording is optional and will depend entirely on your resources, test requirements, and what you plan to do with the recordings. Here are some things to keep in mind.

► **Audio recording:** This is probably the simplest type of test recording you can do. Recording the audio of tests will allow your test facilitator to sit back and listen/observe rather than worry about accurately capturing every action in his or her notes. Audio recordings are also handy to have so you can revisit the test and/or present the test to those who weren't in attendance, such as your web team and library administration. Audio recording is also advisable if you're conducting a focus group to gather feedback from a group of users.

▶ **Video recording:** Also optional, some usability professionals encourage setting up a video camera or a webcam to capture your testers' physical reactions, facial expressions, and so forth.

▶ **Screen recording:** A number of software packages allow you to record screen activity, from basic screencasting applications (such as Camtasia and Captivate) to fully functional usability testing software applications. The former allow you to simply capture screen activity and mouse movements and usually export the results in video format; the latter perform this function as well but also come with varying amounts and types of analytics that analyze screen activity and generalize patterns. For your average usability test, screen recording might be overkill because, chances are, no one is really going to watch screencasts of old tests anyway. But if you do decide that screen recording is essential for your test environment, see Chapter 2, "Screencasting" (p. 10), for a list of screencasting software you can use for this purpose.

Decide Who Should Observe and What They Should Do

Depending on the setup of your test space, you may have the opportunity to install a closed-circuit camera in the room and allow people to observe the test in progress from a remote location. If you do have the ability to set up such a camera and remote viewing location, it's a good idea to open up the observation deck to everyone and anyone involved with your library who has an interest in observing the test. This includes librarians, administrators, other library workers, board members, and Friends of the library. The more people who see how powerful testing is, the more organizational support you'll have for conducting tests in the future. Note that all observers should be remote and not in the room with the facilitator and tester—the last thing your tester needs is an audience.

Test observers should come prepared to watch, take notes, and defer analysis. The latter is probably the most important (and most difficult!) part of the process, because observing a usability test in progress is an extremely enlightening experience, and observers might be tempted to latch on to something they see a single tester doing and making recommendations based on that single activity rather than generalizing all results upon conclusion. We have seen examples, time and again, of observers jumping to conclusions based on observing a single test—for example, just because one tester doesn't see a blue icon does not mean that you should change the color of that icon! Although you will, undoubtedly, be tempted to do so.

Hold a Debrief Meeting

The debrief meeting is a crucial part of the testing process, because it is the time when everyone who observed the tests comes together to discuss what they observed during the testing process. It is at this point when observers gather their notes and thoughts and map out what worked and what didn't work during the testing scenarios. As mentioned previously, there is a great temptation to make changes and fix things right away, but it's important to gather all the evidence and discuss the pain points before making any changes to your site/interface. The debrief meeting is the place where this evidence gathering happens.

Price of Entry

It is important to limit attendance at the debrief meeting to those who actually observed all the tests. If you open up the meeting to non-observers or those who observed only some of the tests you will end up spending too much time summarizing tests for those who weren't in attendance, and you might end up making decisions about changes based on observing only a few tests. To avoid muddying the waters, it is best to include only those who observed all tests in the debrief meeting.

Purpose of Meeting

The debrief meeting is all about summarizing and synthesizing the data from the usability tests. As such, these meetings are usually characterized by a lot of discussion and brainstorming. The first step is to collect a list of all the usability issues into a single document or list.

Our advice is to structure this first step around the tasks performed during the test. In our experience, some of the best debrief meetings make generous use of flip charts and whiteboards placed around the meeting room, with a single page or board devoted to each task. Once your observers have gathered in the meeting room, request them to comb through their notes and add their observations about each of the tasks (from all testers) to the appropriate chart or board. Once everyone has added their comments, the group should reconvene to discuss the comments gathered for each task. The process can take a few hours, depending on the number of tasks performed during the tests and on the number of tests completed, so expect to schedule multiple debrief meetings if necessary. Once all the evidence has been gathered and discussed, the project lead should transcribe the meeting notes in a grid or table that captures each task and all the observed comments for each task.

Once this step has been completed, it is time to turn the discussion to making decisions about what usability problems should be fixed first. While each person at the table might have a different agenda for what needs to be tackled first, it's important to rank the issues on a scale from "critical" to "nice to have" (or some variation thereof).

Deciding what constitutes a critical change is sometimes tricky, but a good rule of thumb to keep in mind is: if it's broken, it's critical. That is to say, if there are actual programming errors that stand in the way of the site/interface working the way it's supposed to, those errors should be fixed first. Beyond these critical issues (which are often the easiest to isolate and fix), the group will have to decide what other usability issues need to be addressed. The list of critical tasks that you came up with prior to testing should help guide the discussion here. If you determined an item to be a critical task, the usability issues uncovered around those tasks should be fixed next.

Inform Others

Spreading the word about what is happening as a result of usability testing is a good way to drum up interest in it. It can also be useful to let others know what your web team is working on and why things change on your website. That being said, creating exhaustive reports about your usability tests isn't necessary. They can take a lot of effort to produce, and most people won't read all of the reports anyway. Instead, spend a few minutes writing an e-mail that summarizes what you tested and why. Include what you learned and what changes you're going to try. You can send this summary to staff who observed the test and participated in the debrief meeting and anyone else who's interested. Be sure to invite folks to the next usability test and assure them there will be snacks.

Guerrillas in the Library

As we've written it, planning for and conducting usability tests is pretty straightforward and simple. Most libraries can make this part of their website development and governance process. If you're even partially responsible for your library's website and don't have the time to do usability testing, make the time by dropping something else. If you can't get administrative or staff support to do testing, you'll need to go guerrilla. Just like we suggested you approach patrons to ask them about what they do on your site, you can also ask people to test your site. Spending as little as five minutes watching patrons use your site can be quite informative.

Conduct Tests Early and Often

It is never too early to start conducting usability tests. If you're thinking about changing something on your website, whether it be a label or adding a new feature, test it before going to the trouble of actually making the change. Although you can, you don't even have to spend the time and effort mocking something up in Photoshop. Don't be afraid to test hand-drawn sketches or wireframes with actual library users. Testing ideas before they are implemented will save your library time and money and perhaps, more importantly, it will iron out kinks in advance and save you from frustrating your patrons. For more on this form of usability testing, see *Paper Prototyping* by Carolyn Snyder (http://www.paperprototyping.com/).

▶ PERFORM A CARD SORT

Card sorts might be the simplest type of usability test you can perform and the results usually provide a trove of rich data that can inform everything from how to label navigation items to how to build the entire architecture of your website. While your average usability test (as described earlier) tests the usability of an interface or website, a card sort actually gets at how your users expect to see your site structured, how items should be grouped, and how those groups should be labeled. That is an amazing amount of rich detail, all for the price of an easy, five-minute test!

As is the case with most usability tests, card sorts can be carried out in both no-tech and high-tech environments. The no-tech version of a card sort actually involves using paper cards, where your testers will move the physical cards into categories and name the categories using paper and pens. The high-tech version of a card sort takes place online, using card sorting software that allows your testers to virtually move cards around, categorize them, and label those categories, all on their screens (see Chapter 2 for a list of card sorting software and online applications). For the purposes of this discussion, we will assume you are doing an in-person, no-tech card sort with your testers. However, keep in mind that the same principles outlined below also apply to any virtual card sorts you might perform with your testers.

There are two types of card sorts you can perform for any site/ interface: open and closed sorts. Depending on the type of information you are looking for from your users, you will probably want to choose one over the other, and you might also perform both as part of a larger website redesign project. Usually open sorts are done first to gauge how users categorize items, and closed sorts are done later to test those categories.

Open Card Sorts

The purpose of an open card sort is to find out how users think about the types of information on your website and how those elements naturally fit together. In an open card sort, you provide testers with website elements (these can be sections, pages, navigation items, etc.) written on index cards and ask them to gather these elements into groups that make sense to them. Your testers will then create descriptions or labels to describe each group they've created.

What emerges from an open card sort will give you an idea of how your users naturally look for certain types of information—thematically, by format, by purpose, by use, by location, and so on and so forth. As you might imagine, the data you gather from a series of open card sorts will give you and your design team a great deal of useful data on how best to construct the architecture of your website.

Closed Card Sorts

While an open card sort would come early in the design process, you would usually perform a closed card sort later in the process. This is because the purpose of a closed card sort is to put your website groupings (or sections, or navigation structure) in front of testers to see if those groupings and labels make sense to them. In a closed card sort, you present two series of index cards to your testers: one series containing elements of your website (call it series A for clarity) and another, smaller, series with the groupings and labels you have already decided upon with one label per card (series B). It is because a closed card sort assumes that you have already made those grouping and label decisions that this type of sort comes later in the design process. Often, a closed card sort will test the results you gathered from the open card sort you performed earlier.

Recruiting for Card Sorts

Recruiting for all usability testing follows the same rules—make sure you recruit from your user population (unless you are specifically looking for input from nonusers), and don't feel the need to perform a lot of tests—five to ten will usually do. When recruiting for card sorts, you usually want to stay within your user population, because the nature of a card sort requires your testers to have some prior knowledge of library website content and functionality. Also, as with other usability tests, you will uncover sufficient data from five to ten tests.

You can carry out a card sorting exercise with both groups of testers and individual testers. In our experience, individual sorting exercises provide the richest data, because individual testers have complete control over the exercise and are therefore unswayed by group ideas and decisions. On the other hand, doing three exercises with three testers takes less time than nine individual card sorting exercises. It will be up to you to weigh the benefit of performing tests with individuals against the amount of time it will take to complete those tests. Once you have facilitated a few sorting exercises, you will probably figure out what works best for you and your website and settle on a preference.

Steps of a Basic Card Sort

Imagine this scenario: you are about halfway through a website redesign project and you and your team have identified and written content for 50 pages that will become part of the new website. The pages represent all the major types of content your users come to the site for (things like library hours, borrowing policies, events, services, resources, and so on). Once you have identified and written these pages, your next step will be to put them online and create a navigation system that provides access to each of them. It is at this stage of the process when you should gather a few testers for an open card sort, because the card sort itself will help you identify what your new navigation structure should be.

To perform the actual sort, begin by taking the names of your 50 pages and writing each out on an index card (one page label per card). The labels you use on the cards should be simple and clear enough for an average user to understand (if you need to explain the label, use the back of the card to do so; also make note of how much explanation each card requires—if you need to explain each label, you're probably using the wrong labels to begin with!). It is important to note that, at this stage, you should perform the sort on items at the same level in the hierarchy on your site—that is, if some of your cards are more granular than others, your testers will have trouble grouping the cards in meaningful ways. Once you have your 50 pages identified on 50 cards, you are ready to begin the test.

As with any usability test, you will begin by providing instructions to your testers. Include the following information in your instructions:

- ▶ Define the purpose of the test.
- ▶ Describe what you hope to get out of the results.
- ▶ Clarify your role during the test.
- ▶ Remind them that they are not being tested! There are no right and wrong answers to the card sort—you are simply seeking input to inform the final organization of your site.
- ▶ Ask them to organize the cards into groups that make sense to them.
- ▶ For an open card sort, request your testers to label or describe each group once they have finished doing the grouping; remember to provide sufficient blank cards for your testers to use for the labeling portion of the sort.
- ▶ For a closed card sort, provide your testers with a series of cards with each of your labels clearly printed on a card (series A) in addition to the series of website elements or pages (series B); instruct your testers to place series A in front of them and lay out the cards from series B that they think should belong to each label in series A.
- ▶ For both types of card sorts, let your users know that they can create a "miscellaneous" pile for cards that they don't know how to categorize.

For the rest of the test, your role as facilitator will be to stand back and observe the card sort in action. It is a good idea to observe where your sorters get hung up and which cards they end up moving to multiple groups before deciding on a final home. Once your sorters have completed the task, spend a few minutes debriefing the sort with them. Ask them which cards they had trouble with and any other observations they might have about the task.

Sample Closed Card Sort Instructions

Thank you for taking the time to do this test. The purpose of the exercise is to help us determine if the people who use our website (like you!) can find their way around the navigation options we've used. So, it's important for me to tell you that you aren't in any way being tested! Instead, we're interested to know if the choices we've made for our website make sense to you. If they don't, we plan to make changes based on the results of this test and a few others. So, there are no right and wrong answers here.

(Continued)

(Continued)

I have two series of cards: series A and series B. Series A are some categories, and series B are items that I'd like you to look at and figure out which category in series A it falls under. Again, there are no right and wrong answers! We just want to see if these categories and names make sense to you and how you would organize the options in series B. If anything in series B doesn't make sense to you and you can't figure out which category to put it under, don't worry about it. Just set it aside in this "miscellaneous," pile and we'll talk about that pile when you're all done.

So, my role now is to just make sure that you understand these instructions and step aside and let you get categorizing! Do you have any questions? Also, feel free to talk this out as you work on the exercise.

Analyzing Card Sorting Data

The best possible result of a card sort would be 100 percent agreement from all testers, but the likelihood of this happening is slim to none! Therefore, you will probably have to perform some analysis of the results you collect during your card sort exercises. As with most usability data, there is no science to analyzing the results of a card sort exercise. Once you have conducted a number of card sorts, you will begin to see patterns emerge from the results, and it is these patterns that will provide you with most of the information you need on how to make use of the test results.

The most efficient way to analyze card sorting data is to create a spreadsheet to record the raw data. On a single worksheet, enter the card labels from series B in the first column and enter the labels from series A in the first row. Note that in an open sort, these will differ for each sort, so you will need multiple worksheets to accomplish this; in a closed sort, these will be the labels you came up with yourself, so one worksheet should do. Once you have your first column and row filled in, work across the table entering the number of times each card was placed under each label. Entering in the raw data can take a bit of time, but the process is an extremely useful one because you will begin to see patterns emerge as you complete the data entry. For a sample spreadsheet that you can use for card sort data, check the companion website for this series (http://www.alatechsource.org/techset/).

Once you have isolated the patterns in your card sort results, you should take some time to look at the outliers, or those cards/elements that resulted in the least agreement among your testers. The outliers often provide the most telling data because these are the website elements that are the most problematic. There are a number of possible reasons why testers largely disagree on the placement of these outliers, including a lack of understanding of the label used on the card and the possibility that the element itself is too broad/general to pin down to one specific category. It's a good idea to spend some time reviewing the outliers, brainstorming possible reasons why testers couldn't agree on them, and making changes accordingly. Then complete the process by conducting another card sort to test the validity of your assumptions.

▶ CREATE PERSONAS

What Are Personas?

Personas are fictional depictions of your website's target audiences. They can be a cornerstone of your website planning process and should have an ongoing role as you evolve your site.

Personas aren't real people. They're composite character sketches that result from researching real people. Although personas usually include some basic demographic information, they're much more than a market research–based demographic audience segmentation. With the latter, a library might state that one type of library user is a male, aged 12–18. A persona will include that information but will also go deeper, describing an audience's behaviors, motivations, needs, and goals.

Why Use Personas?

Understanding library users is an essential component of creating a user-centered website. It is impossible to design something for someone you know nothing about. Developing personas is a way to accumulate knowledge about users and develop empathy for them. The resulting persona document is a reminder of your research process and your organization's increased understanding of its users.

Personas help ensure that library staff agree who it is, exactly, that you're building your website for. This is useful because it highlights the fact that you're designing for actual library users, not librarians. Ideally, your web team will make design decisions based on your understanding of these people, not random preferences. Have you ever been in a website planning session and heard someone make a suggestion based on their personal preferences? Have you ever heard someone say something like, "It would be really cool if we put that on the site?" Personas can elevate the discussion, help you make better decisions, and move the conversation away from the personal preferences of members of the web team. The success of your website hinges on understanding your target audience and creating a relevant destination.

How to Develop Personas

Step 1: Conduct User Research

Because personas are representations of the people you're trying to serve, it is imperative that you learn about those people. An effective way to do this is through user interviews.

Planning Interviews

Before you can actually interview people you'll need to decide who you're going to talk with. A good place to start would be with a typical demographic audience segmentation. Your personas will eventually give you a deeper understanding of your community than the average demographic data, but you need to start your planning somewhere. Instead of simply dividing your patrons into children, teens, and adults or into undergrads, grad students, and faculty, find unique things about the folks your library serves. Perhaps your community has a significant percentage of senior citizens or distance education students. Make sure those groups are represented by some of the people you interview. Find two to four people to interview for each audience segment, and schedule your interviews.

Conducting Interviews

User interviews are guided and open-ended conversations. If you've worked a reference desk before, this might sound familiar. User interviews are very similar to reference interviews. The aim is to get the other person talking without biasing his or her responses. But where reference interviews are about a particular learning need, what are discussed during user interviews are people's lives. Just like during reference interviews, make your conversation partners feel comfortable. Ensure them that there are no correct or incorrect responses and that they should be open and honest about their goals and needs.

As tempting as it might be, it's important to avoid directly asking interviewees about their library use. Remember, you're attempting to learn about their behaviors, lives, motivations, and goals, not what they like or don't like about your library. Here are some sample questions and statements to start or redirect a conversation or to use when there's a lull in conversation:

- ▶ Tell me about your reading habits.
- ▶ What do you do when you want to watch a movie?
- ▶ What is your research process like?
- ▶ Do you buy books? If so, what kind, and why?
- ▶ Tell me about what you do when you need to find information on a topic or subject.

The interview isn't a time to do analysis, but if anything you hear sparks your interest, make a note of it and ask, "Tell me more about that" or "Why do you do that?"

You can take extensive notes throughout the conversation, but it isn't recommended. It is the faster and less expensive option, but it can stifle the conversation's flow, and you'll miss important bits. Instead, consider getting permission to record the interviews. You can then transcribe the conversation or employ a transcribing service. A third alternative is to have another librarian take notes during the conversation, in the same room or remotely.

Step 2: Analyze Research

The most time-consuming part of the user research process is reviewing your transcripts or notes and pulling out all the behaviors your interview subjects reported. Once you have a master list of behaviors, group similar behaviors together thematically. This will take a lot of time, but it provides you with an invaluable opportunity to get to the heart of your users' behaviors, needs, goals, and motivations. As a solo activity, it can be long and arduous, which is why it's a great activity to get your web committee involved in, too. Once you have your thematically grouped list of behaviors, you have the raw material from which you will develop your personas.

Shoestring Budget Persona Development

Although the resulting documents won't be nearly as accurate or valuable, it is possible to create personas without talking to community members. Interviewing even a few people is better than interviewing none, but if you want to create personas quickly, here's how.

(Continued)

(Continued)

Do the same audience segmentation as if you were going to interview people. But instead of conducting user interviews, lead a brainstorming session with your staff. Ask the same questions you'd ask of real community members, and ask staff to respond as if they're the interview subject. Encourage people to make "I" statements, because it will help them think like other people. If you ask, "Tell me about your reading habits," they might respond with "I read in the morning when no one else in my house is awake" or "I end up skimming most articles I set aside." Plan to spend 45 minutes to an hour brainstorming behaviors for each audience segment.

Record the statements on a whiteboard or flip chart so that you can then group similar behaviors into your personas.

Step 3: Create Persona Documents

You have gathered the raw material for each of your personas. Now it is time to fill in the details. Think of creating a persona as if you're writing miniature biographies or snapshots of someone's life. In addition to writing about their library related needs, you should include other little slices of their life to flesh out the character and render him or her believable.

Name

Personas can come alive and be more effective when you give them a first name. Plus, it is more memorable and easier to refer to "Kelly" than it is to refer to the generic "young researcher" or "older reader." Brainstorm appropriate names, and consider using some descriptors. Names like "William the Reader" and "Scott the Searcher" increase memorability and help fill in the character.

Photograph

When aiming to make your personas realistic and lifelike, including photos of your personas is a must. Make sure the photos fit the characters, matching their demographic characteristics and attitudes. Not all photos work as well as others, and the best are often yearbook-style head and shoulder shots. Don't use photos of celebrities, library workers, or library users. Use realistic photos of normal people.

Finding the right photograph can take some time. Searching Flickr (http://flickr.com/) for Creative Commons licensed photos can be effective, but we've had a better time using iStockphoto (http://istockphoto.com/) and morgueFile (http://morguefile.com/).

Key Differences

You'll want a clear way to summarize what makes each persona unique. List one to three of the most important needs, desires, or characteristics. Descriptions could be anything from "Enjoys ample leisure time" to "Trying to make ends meet" to "Focused on his kids."

Gender

You might have a gut instinct whether to make a persona male or female. If the decision doesn't seem obvious, think back to the people you interviewed from which your persona's characteristics came. Were they mostly male or female? If this still doesn't help, it is likely unimportant which gender a particular persona should be. Choose one that will make your group of personas diverse. If you choose an appropriate name and photograph, you won't have to state the persona's gender explicitly.

Age

Public libraries serve people of all ages. The range of ages that academic and special libraries serve is narrower. Unless you plan on excluding an age group, it's a good idea to create personas that reflect the diversity of ages you serve. Be careful when assigning ages, though. You don't want this to have too significant of an impact on your persona development, because you'll run the risk of creating the typical library market audience segmentations. Remember, audience segments and personas aren't the same things.

Quote

Including a short quote for each persona helps in humanizing the character and fleshes out his or her characteristics and goals. Consider this example of a persona for a college library:

> "I'm all over campus. Sometimes I work in one of the computer labs, sometimes I'm looking for good WiFi, and sometimes I'm too exhausted to go anywhere so I do research in my dorm room."

This quote highlights the goals, motivations, and values of this persona.

Goals

A persona's goals might be the single most important part of the persona document. This is because user motivations and goals should be the focal point for your web development, so you need to ensure that the goals of each persona represent actual user goals within your community. When writing goals for each persona, make sure to include both experience goals and end goals. Experience goals provide an indication of how the persona wants to feel when using your website, and end goals indicate what the persona would like to accomplish on the site. Here is a typical set of goals for a persona using a library intranet:

1. Connect with other library staff members. (experience goal)
2. Input vacation time for HR purposes. (end goal)
3. Find insurance claim forms. (end goal)

In addition to goals, consider including some of the following to help develop your personas and make them more human:

- ▶ Occupation
- ▶ Education
- ▶ Web skills
- ▶ Websites often visited
- ▶ Hobbies

A final word of caution about developing your personas: it is easy to get caught up fleshing out the biographical details of each of your personas—giving them personal characteristics, filling in their biographical details, giving them a history and attitudes—because these are fun activities that appeal to the novelist in us all! As much as these characteristics will help you forge a connection with your personas as you learn more about them (which is important when developing for them), make sure you don't get bogged down with these details. Instead, focus the majority of your time and energy on figuring out their needs and goals. A good way to do this is to begin with a brief biographical sketch (name, age, and gender), then spend the bulk of your persona development time filling in the goals and needs, and, only when you are happy with those details, turn your attention to adding any of the other characteristics you need to complete the persona (quote, occupation, etc.).

Document Design

Although many UX practitioners love exercising their graphic design chops creating them, persona documents don't need to be fancy. Whatever program you use to create your personas, use a template. You can make a template yourself, or use one of the many readily available on the web. Figure 5.1 provides an example created in Microsoft Word.

▶ Figure 5.1: Persona Document

Stacy the Scanner

Gender	Female
Age	36
Education	Bachelors of Science
Occupation	Homemaker
Hobbies	Tennis, raising 2 kids

"I need to get the maximum value I can from anything I do. Efficiency is king."

Story

Being a stay-at-home-mom is all about planning and patience! Every moment of every day is planned because it has to be -- there is a lot to get done and all sorts of appointments to remember, from chores to homework to after-school activities that the kids are involved in. I like to keep the kids busy, but I also really need to figure out ways to find some time for myself during the day, so I try to schedule family activities that we can all participate in, but I also try to find some downtime for myself, where I can read a book or meet a friend for coffee or something like that. It's a sanity break that is really necessary, but often difficult to fit into our busy lives.

Goals

- Provide the best for her kids

- Carve out some "me time" during the busy week

Key Differences

- Purpose driven

- Spends money for convenience

- Routine oriented

In addition to creating individual personas, consider creating an overview document with some of the most important details (see Figure 5.2). Tape up your overview document in staff workrooms and at desks to serve as a gentle but constant reminder of your users and their needs.

How to Use Personas

You've learned a lot about your community through the persona development process. Now you can put some of this knowledge to use. The following process will help you figure out how your website can meet your community's needs and goals.

Step 1: Brainstorm Ideas

Spend time talking about each persona, thinking of what they need from a library website. List responses on a flip chart, or, ideally, write each idea on a sticky note and group them together. Be very mindful of the type of brainstorming you're doing by focusing on these very different questions. Answer them one by one, using different colored sticky notes for each question. Note that your website might already contain some of the ideas you're coming up with. That's okay.

▶ Figure 5.2: Persona Overview Document

Persona Overview Document

Stacy the Scanner

Gender	Female
Age	36
Education	Bachelors of Science
Occupation	Homemaker
Hobbies	Tennis, raising 2 kids

Quote
"I need to get the maximum value I can from anything I do. Efficiency is king."

Goals
- Provide the best for her kids
- Carve out some "me time" during the busy week

Key Differences
- Purpose driven
- Spends money for convenience
- Routine oriented

Fun Frank

Gender	Male
Age	65
Education	MBA
Occupation	Retired
Hobbies	Golf, cooking

Quote
"Why not? I've got the time."

Goals
- Entertain his friends more
- Stay healthy

Key Differences
- Has ample free time
- Financially secure
- Likes to stay close to home

Tom the Tinkerer

Gender	Male
Age	27
Education	High school
Occupation	Sales rep
Hobbies	Riding bicycles

Quote
"I try things and see what happens."

Goals
- Open a sporting goods store
- Do more adventure travel

Key Differences
- Budget-conscious
- Spontaneous
- Ambitious

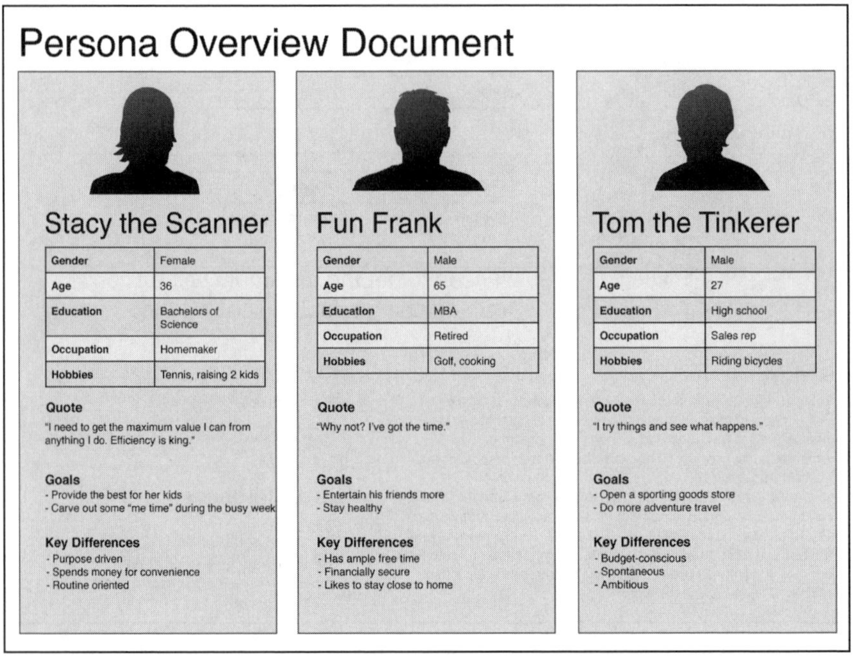

▶ **What does X need from the library in order to be successful in life?** This emphasizes the life of the persona and his or her needs. It is the most important question of the three.

▶ **What does X need in order to successfully use the library?** This emphasizes the persona's actual and potential library use, narrowing the focus of the brainstorming.

▶ **What might X want from the library?** This also emphasizes the persona's actual and potential library use but moves the discussion from necessities to "nice to haves."

The sky is the limit during these brainstorming sessions. Although they'll come into play later, no one should be thinking about limitations at this point. Instead, the classic "there are no wrong answers" brainstorming rule applies. This is an opportunity to develop your creative thinking skills.

You might find that during the brainstorming process it is very easy to fall into the trap of projecting your goals, as librarians and library workers, onto your personas, so make sure to keep your personas at the forefront of your mind and remind your team members to do the same. This is often more difficult to accomplish than you might realize, especially when you have already put a lot of time and effort into developing various parts of your website. A classic example we have come across is for a subject librarian to assume that the music undergraduate would like a great subject guide for music resources. In truth, the music undergraduate probably just wants to be able to find resources for his or her research easily and might not even know that the music subject guide exists (or what a subject guide is at all)! So, beware of projecting your goals onto your personas, and remind your team members that you are trying to come up with end users' goals, not what you *hope* or *would like* your users to want or need from their library!

Step 2: Prioritize Ideas

After you've brainstormed ideas for each persona, go back through each list and rank the ideas. Ask the group which ideas best meet the needs of the persona, and reorder the list so that the best ideas are at the top. Ideas that aren't as inspiring or just plain wrong can go to the bottom or be erased.

Step 3: Plan

Congratulations! Now you know the most important things to include on your website for different parts of your community. But you're not done quite yet. The final step of this process involves comparing your current website to the ideas you've just generated and ranked. Go through your lists a final time to determine what you need to do and when you're going to do it. Record answers to the following questions in a spreadsheet:

> ▶ Are we already doing this?
> ▶ If we're already doing this, can we improve it?
> ▶ Should we pursue this idea now or later?

Now is the time to start thinking about how these ideas intersect with the resources you have available. For instance, you might have brainstormed that one of your personas would use daily personalized article recommendations. As good an idea as this might be, it might be impossible for you to do at the moment because of technology and staff limitations. This would be an idea to pursue later. On the other hand, an idea that isn't as important might be very easy to accomplish. Do it right away for a quick win.

You will probably need to spend at least an hour on each of these steps. These meetings tend to take up as much time as you give them, so watch the clock carefully. Give people breaks every 45 minutes to keep them fresh and motivated.

Beyond Brainstorming

Personas don't lose their value once you've used them to brainstorm ideas and assess your website. They should become your trusted sources whenever you're making decisions about your website or other library services.

Get everyone in the habit of referring to personas when talking about new content or features. A statement such as "We should have information about our book discussion groups because Randy is looking to socialize and learn" is a great starting point from which to discuss creating content. By creating a reference point, personas give everyone a meaningful way to talk about website ideas.

If suggestions about your website aren't so well formed and don't include references to relevant personas, you can use personas to test the suggestion. If it is difficult to figure out which of your personas would use this new content or feature, it should immediately be suspect. Remember, personas represent actual users. So, not being able to find a persona that would use, say, a movie review podcast means that you're unable to find a significant group of real users who would use this content. Conversely, ideas that appeal to all or most personas should be given high priority when it comes to development time.

Common Questions about Personas

How Do I Know If My Personas Are Good?

They Are Realistic

After you've created a persona, ask people-oriented frontline library workers to look it over. Check in with them to see if one or two real-life examples of this persona come to mind. If they immediately say, "Oh, yeah, this is like Mr. Smith who comes in on Tuesday afternoons," you know you're on target. If they struggle to identify an actual library patron who matches your persona, consider it a red flag.

They Differ

If someone reads a few bits of an individual persona to you, can you guess who they're talking about? Your personas shouldn't blend together. Because they represent different users with different needs, it should be easy to distinguish among them. They should be as different from each other as the people you serve.

They Are Comprehensive

If you think of library patrons who don't fit any of your personas you may be missing an important audience. Did you exclude a group during your brainstorming or interviews?

They Are Being Used

The best personas teach library staff about patrons and how the library can meet their needs. If created with care, the personas will be compelling enough to engage people and increase empathy for patrons.

How Many Personas Should I Create?

There's no one-size-fits-all answer to this question. The number of personas you need to create will depend on what your research data tell you. In our experience it will likely be more than three, but if you create more than seven personas there will most likely be overlap in their goals and needs. If there's too much overlap, the personas are probably too granular and might lose their distinctiveness and power. Consider combining them.

Should Personas Describe Potential Library Users or Actual Library Users?

Ah, a trick question. Don't think of developing personas in terms of users versus nonusers. During the development phase it doesn't matter whether these folks are using your library or not. What matters is that you paint an accurate picture of who they are and what they need. You'll get a sense of whether or not these folks are current library users when you compare your current website offerings to their needs.

Keep Personas Alive

Remember, persona documents are the result of a deliberate research process. As such, they should be adaptable and fluid. When your library learns more about the needs of your community, make sure that knowledge gets folded into the personas. Consider keeping a file of additional accumulated bits of library patron information. Review the file occasionally to see if there is anything new, compelling, supporting, or contradictory. Investigate further and adjust your personas accordingly.

Get Comfortable with Your Personas

You might feel silly at first referring to these fictional characters by their names, but hopefully you will get over it. Just remember that your personas' names are a shorthand way to refer to specific target audiences and user groups.

▶ PERFORM A HEURISTIC EVALUATION OF YOUR WEBSITE

When you've spent a lot of time working on a website it can be difficult to see it with fresh eyes. This is one reason why usability testing is so important; it provides a fresh perspective. Another way to leave bias behind is to compare a site to web conventions and best practices. This is called a heuristic evaluation, and it can be an effective way to determine the overall health of a site and to identify areas to improve.

Conducting a Heuristic Evaluation

Consider your site compared to the checkpoints listed below and assign your site a score. We recommend the following scale:

−1 = Site does not comply.
0 = Site is somewhat compliant.
1 = Site is fully compliant.

Using a scale with more granularity only confuses things. The difference between a 0 and 1 is much more obvious than, say, the difference between a 4 and 5.

Keep track of the scores in a spreadsheet that you can review after completing the evaluation. You can download a spreadsheet of these checkpoints from the companion website for this series (http://www.alatechsource.org/techset/).

The following are some areas of your site you'll want to evaluate.

Visual Design

- ▶ Pages aren't crammed full of text and images. Whitespace is used effectively.
  Why: Less content renders the content that's there easier to read.
- ▶ Page titles and headings are anchored and not floating (see Figure 5.3).
  Why: This gives the page an appropriate rhythm and makes information easy to skim.

▶ Figure 5.3: Template for Visual Design

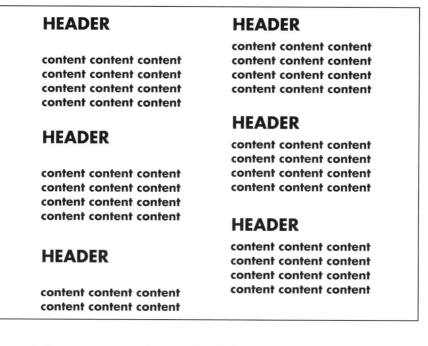

▶ Colors are appropriate and well designed.

Why: They make sites easier to read, and a well-designed site increases the amount of trust users have for it.

Navigation

▶ The navigational structure is broad rather than deep.

Why: It is easy to get lost in websites with many layers.

▶ Navigation is persistent.

Why: This helps orient users and provides consistent options.

▶ Paths to critical content and tasks are obvious and clear.

Why: It is more important to provide obvious paths rather than to make sure that all of your site's content should be available in a certain number of clicks.

▶ The website is organized to support the most important information patrons need and the tasks they want to accomplish.

Why: Organizing according to your library's organizational structure is library focused and less useful to users.

▶ Avoid library jargon for labels.

Why: Phrases like "Readers' Advisory" are meaningless to patrons. Test labels with patrons to see what they understand.

▶ The site is orienting.

Why: Make sure your site provides feedback about where people are in the site. They should be able to understand what section of the site they're in and what subsection. Consistent use of breadcrumbs helps (see Figure 5.4).

▶ Include a catalog search box on the homepage.

Why: This is the number one task people want to accomplish, so it should be easy. Don't make people hunt for a catalog search box.

Content

Images

▶ Do not use clip art.

Why: At best it simply adds no value. Usually it creates cluttered pages.

▶ Do not use stock photos.

Why: They're generally perceived as generic and inauthentic. Instead, use high-quality photographs of your library, library workers, and patrons.

▶ Do not use images for text.

Why: The words can't be copied and pasted, and they can't be read by screen readers.

▶Figure 5.4: Nestlé's Global Corporate Website Orienting Users

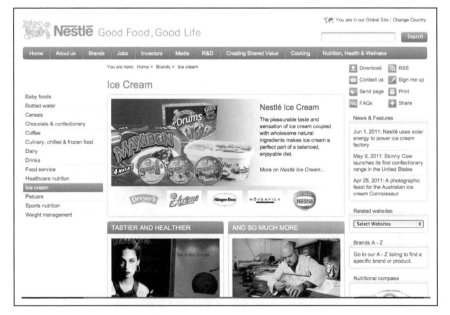

▶ Use PDFs appropriately.

Why: Remember that you're mostly providing information, not documents. HTML is a much more user-friendly and faster way to give people information. Use PDFs only when you're providing a document that people will want to read all of or that has special formatting needs.

Writing

▶ Content goes through an editorial process.

Why: Even the best writers need editing. Don't write something and publish it immediately. Don't make it difficult for writing to get edited, approved, and published.

▶ Someone is assigned to review content on a regular basis.

Why: Content must be reviewed to ensure it is still relevant. It won't happen magically, so someone needs to be responsible for doing this.

▶ Don't retain content that isn't being used.

Why: It just gets in the way of people finding stuff they want. Remove everything that isn't important.

▶ Content isn't created indiscriminately.

Why: Everything on your website should deliberately meet a library or user need.

▶ Content isn't written in an institutional voice.

Why: Writing with a human voice is friendlier.

▶ Content isn't written in the passive voice.

Why: The active voice is more engaging.

Example

Passive and institutional: Tests can be proctored by the library.

Active and friendly: We can proctor tests for you.

▶ Refer to your library as "we" and patrons as "you." If writing from a patron's perspective, use "I."

Why: This is friendly and humanizing.

Example

"Resetting PINs"
Patrons can visit a library location to have their PIN reset. They can also click here to reset it online.
   versus:
How do I reset my pin?
You can reset your PIN online or visit a library in person.

► Avoid using "click here" or "more" for links.
Why: Meaningful text helps users.

Example

Read <u>more</u> at our Calendar of Events.
versus:
Read more at our <u>Calendar of Events</u>.

► Information is in chunks that are easy to skim.
Why: Long paragraphs are impenetrable.
► Use bulleted lists where effective.
Why: They're easy to skim.

Using the Heuristic Evaluation

Once you've rated your site, scroll around the resulting spreadsheet to see your site's strengths and weaknesses. Develop a plan for turning the −1s and 0s into 1s.

► CREATE A CONTENT STRATEGY

Content: Why It Is on Your Site

While your website's appearance is important, a site's looks aren't enough to satisfy someone on a mission. A library website that's extremely attractive and well organized will still be a failure if the content isn't relevant to its users.

In a presentation at South by Southwest (SXSW) on March 12, 2010, Margot Bloomstein (http://www.slideshare.net/mbloomstein/content-strategy-whats-in-it-for-you-at-sxsw) compared the content on a website to most spice cabinets. Think of the collection of spices in your library's kitchen. You have a general idea of what's there, but you don't have encyclopedic knowledge of what's available. You're not sure when it got there, how it got there, or if anyone is using any of it. You don't know of a plan to get more. And, importantly, you don't know for sure how fresh the spices are and if any of them are worth using. The same thing applies to many library websites. Does it sound familiar to you?

Because content is the real reason people visit a website, why is it often neglected by libraries (and other institutions too)? Libraries often spend so much effort sorting out the technical aspects of maintaining a website that there's not room for much else. And we've all done so much writing in our lives that it seems like a no brainer or like a piece of the puzzle that can be plugged in at any time. After all, writing is easy, right? Wrong. Good, relevant content takes hard work to create and maintain.

Don't fret if the spice cabinet scenario feels familiar. There's a systematic assessment method that you can use to learn about what's on your website: a content audit.

Conducting a Content Audit

Conducting a content audit involves looking at every piece of content on your website—not just every webpage but also every PDF, audio file, video file, and image. Ideally you'll have multiple people working on the audit, and you all will have the time and motivation to look at every single piece of content on the site. This might seem excessive, but the result will certainly highlight the enormity of your website and content. This can be useful when you need to convince people to take content creation and maintenance seriously. This could be a big task, yes. But if it isn't important enough to assess, why is it important enough to have on your website?

Catalogers rejoice! The first step of a content audit is to look at the stuff quantitatively. You're essentially going to be cataloging your website in a big spreadsheet (see Figure 5.5). Each piece of content should have a unique page number and some basic information: the page's title, URL, and file type. List the pages in a column on the left and the attributes in the top row. Software such as the free iGooMap can help automate this. This will tell you what stuff is on your site (is it more than you expected?). It is a necessary first step, but it isn't

▶ Figure 5.5: Content Audit

::::	A	B	C
1	**PAGE ID**	**URL**	**NAME**
2	1.0	http://uxlibrary.org	home page
3	1.1	http://uxlibrary.org/research	Research
4	1.2	http://uxlibrary.org/reading	Reading
5	1.2.1	http://uxlibrary.org/reading/comics	Comic Books
6	1.2.2	http://uxlibrary.org/reading/classics	Classics
7	1.3	http://uxlibrary.org/cafe	Library Cafe

enough. Next you'll want to continue the audit with some qualitative assessment in order to learn *about* the content you just cataloged.

You can measure many different things about a piece of content and keep the scale simple. Not only is assigning a 0, 1, or 2 to a piece of content easy, such a course scale will also give you all the information you need when analyzing the content audit. If you can, have the same person complete each column, the one exception being the accuracy column (discussed later). This will provide more consistent measurement. Here are some metrics you can use to assess your site's content.

Creator

▶ What you're assessing: If possible, note who created this piece of content.

▶ What to enter: Name and title.

Responsibility

▶ What you're assessing: Someone different from the person who created a piece of content might be responsible for maintaining it. It can be useful to explicitly state who is responsible for what content.

▶ What to enter: Name and title.

Considerations: If you find it difficult to figure out who is responsible for maintaining particular pieces of content on your library's site, you might want to bring this up to your web team. Clearly delineated content production roles will help when new content needs to be created or when content needs to be updated.

Use

▶ What you're assessing: Do people look at this content? How many page hits has it received?

▶ What to enter: A numeric value (0–2):

0 = This content is rarely used.

1 = This content is among the least visited.

2 = This content receives an average amount of visits.

3 = This content is among the most visited.

4 = This is the most popular content on the website.

Considerations: You'll want to use a data sample that spans a relatively long period of time, perhaps 12 months. Six months would be the minimum. If you don't currently use web analytics software you can install a free tool like Google Analytics to start.

Notice that this scale is a bit larger than the others. Depending on the range of hits you're recording you might want to make this more or less granular. Assign a range of page hits to each numeric value. For instance:

    0 = This content is rarely used (0–2,000 hits per 12 months).
    1 = This content is among the least visited (2,001–4,000 hits per month).

Usefulness to Library

▶ What you're assessing: Is this content useful to the library? Is there a motivation for the library to have this content on the website?
▶ What to enter: A numeric value (0–2):

    0 = This content is not extremely useful.
    1 = This content is useful.
    2 = This content is essential to the website.

Considerations: This is one of the few times in this book that we'll ask you to specifically not think about the needs of library patrons. Think of what the library needs. For instance, whether or not patrons need this content, most libraries have the need for their policies to be on the website. Some libraries have the need for non-English content on their sites. An embedded video, on the other hand, might not have any utility for the library but it may (or may not!) be useful for library patrons. Think of library needs as nuts and bolts business needs. Library stakeholders will be good at assessing whether something is useful for the library to have on the site.

Usefulness to Patrons

▶ What you're assessing: Is this content useful to the library users? Does it solve a problem for library users?
▶ What to enter: A numeric value (0–2):

    0 = This content is not extremely useful.
    1 = This content is useful.
    2 = This content is essential to the website.

Considerations: This is an important column in the audit, and it takes an empathetic mind. How is a librarian supposed to judge whether something is useful for library patrons? Ideally you'll have personas that you can employ to help (see "Create Personas" earlier in this chapter). When examining a piece of content, ask yourself, "Which of our personas would use this content? How important would it be for them?" If you have trouble matching a persona to the content, the content should score no higher than a 1. If you have trouble matching and the content proves to not be important to the persona, it should probably score a 0. Conversely, if all or most audience types would use a piece of content, it might receive a 2. If you haven't yet developed personas, you can still imagine typical library users as you assess the usefulness of content. Remember, you're not judging whether a piece of content could possibly be used sometimes or would be nice to have. You're judging whether this content meets users' core needs.

Web Written

- ▶ What you're assessing: Is this page written for the web? Is the content easily scannable?
- ▶ What to enter: A numeric value (0–2):

  0 = The content reads like a novel and is difficult to scan. It is not presented in a grab-and-go format.

  1 = The content has some appropriate headings and it can be scanned, but it can be tuned up or presented in an easier-to-read format.

  2 = The content is as concise and engaging as possible.

Accuracy

- ▶ What you're assessing: Is the information correct? Up-to-date? Do all the links work?
- ▶ What to enter: A numeric value (0–2):

  0 = There are significant errors about important things.

  1 = There are errors on the page.

  2 = The content is 100 percent accurate.

Considerations: This is the only column that will preferably be filled out by more than one person. Subject matter experts will know whether something is accurate or not. So, someone from Youth Services should assess the pages meant for children and parents, someone from the Reference department should assess reference pages, and so forth.

User Friendly

- ▶ What you'll be assessing: Is this page as easy to use as it could be?
- ▶ What to enter: A numeric value (0–2) and specific commentary:

  0 = This is organization focused and could be made easier to use.

  1 = This is generally easy to use but could be improved.

  2 = This is patron focused and is easy to use.

Considerations: This is a slightly more subjective measurement that's best done by someone with a keen critical eye. This column could contain big ideas like "Printable library card application could be an online form" or small issues like "Text is too small."

Last Date Reviewed

▶ What you'll be assessing: When the content was reviewed.
▶ What to enter: The date of reviewing the content.

Last Updated

▶ What you'll be assessing: When the content was last updated.
▶ What to enter: The date of updating the content.

Accessibility

▶ What you'll be assessing: Whether or not the content passes an accessibility checker.
▶ What to enter: A numeric value (0 or 1):

0 = This content does not comply with accessibility standards.
1 = This content complies with accessibility standards.

Analyzing the Audit

Once you fill out your spreadsheet you'll be able to sort columns to get some clear instructions about what you can do to improve your site. Using the data sort feature in Excel or Numbers, sort multiple columns at the same time. By doing this you can lump together content that has particular combined scores. Here are some useful ways you can sort the data in your spreadsheet.

Used and Inaccurate

Fix these pages immediately! This content might be misinformation, not a good thing to be serving people on a mission.

Used and Not Web Written

Rewriting these pages could be a relatively easy win. Fixing these pages probably won't require technical intervention, just good writing skills. Because they're being used, it would be a good idea to put them high on the priority list.

Unused and Unnecessary

You might consider these pages losers. They are of no use to people or to the library, and no one is looking at them. The biggest risk in removing these pages could be helping the creators of the content understand why it isn't appropriate for the website.

Useful to Patrons and Unused

If these pieces of content are indeed useful for patrons, consider ways to make them used. If it seems that the content is already ideally arranged or it isn't possible to improve their arrangement, like most unused content, it should be considered for removal. Because it has been deemed useful, keep track of this content for possible reintroduction when appropriate.

Useful to Library and Unused

Content that is useful to the library but is not being used should be examined to make sure it truly is useful to the library. If its utility to the library is not related to it being published for patrons to read (e.g., library policies), you should ensure that it isn't getting in the way of user-focused content. If it is, consider moving the content to your staff intranet. This will increase the site's signal to noise ratio and enable users to find content they want with greater ease.

Most Popular Content

Scrutinize these pages further. They're getting the most screen time, so you'll want to make sure they're in top shape. Make sure they're easy to use, visually appealing, and web written.

Least Popular Content

Site analytics can be tricky to interpret. Page hits don't tell us much about site visitors' motivation for being on a certain page or not visiting certain pages. Pages could get skipped because either the content isn't interesting or something is preventing someone from finding the page.

Page hits report that people visited certain pages, but they do not report people's motivations or why they visited the pages. People end up on webpages because:

- ► there is content on the page they want,
- ► the website's information architecture leads them to the page,
- ► the visual design of the site leads them to the page, and/or
- ► the page is an appealing result in a web search.

While a lack of visits doesn't necessarily mean that a page isn't valuable, it does mean that it probably won't be missed if it were to be removed. Use these stats judiciously.

You should examine the least popular pages and attempt to determine if they aren't being used because the pages are hidden by confusing or too deep information architecture or because people simply aren't interested in the content.

By looking at the page IDs you probably notice that many of the unused pages are deep in the website's structure. While it is not possible to say with 100 percent certainty that this correlation is causation, it stands to reason that people won't look at this deep and buried content no matter what's there.

Ongoing Content Audit

Be sure you update the content audit when you improve a piece of content. Even if you manage to turn all of the 0s in the spreadsheet to 2s, there's still more that can be done with the content audit. Ideally you'll change it to reflect changes made to the site, and use it to plan additional reviews and tweaks to the site.

▶ ARRANGE CONTENT WORK FLOW

No matter the size of your organization it will be helpful to have a clearly defined content work flow. It is easier to optimize the work flow or troubleshoot problems when everyone understands how content moves through the organization. Depending on the size and structure of your organization this process may involve just a few people or many people.

The Basic Content Life Cycle

One way to create a work flow is to illustrate the life cycle of a piece of content: how content gets requested, created, edited, published, and removed (see Figure 5.6). Easy enough, right? But creating an illustration like this is only the start. The real work comes when it's time to figure out the human element. There are questions you must answer to sort out who is actually going to do this stuff.

- ▶ **Published:** Who moves content from draft status to being live on the web? When does this happen?
- ▶ **Created:** Who actually creates the content once it is cleared for creation?
- ▶ **Requested:** Who can request content, and how do they do it? Who approves or denies their request?

► Figure 5.6: Basic Content Life Cycle

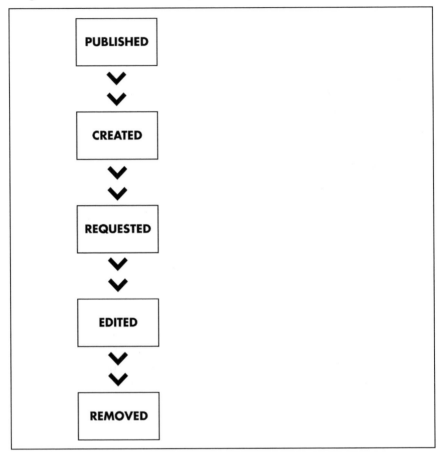

- ► **Edited:** Who will ensure this content is appropriately written for the web?
- ► **Removed:** Who decides when content is no longer appropriate or valuable? Does it get deleted or should it be archived?

Content Roles

Because most libraries don't have the staff capacity to have dedicated full-time employees to do each of the things necessary to take a piece of content through its life cycle, it is often helpful to create content roles.

Content roles are flexible in that sometimes more than one person will fill a role. Especially in smaller institutions, some people will fill more than one role. You might be tempted to combine roles together if one individual is going to be filling more than one, but resist the urge. It is still worthwhile to define distinct roles. This helps everyone not only understand different parts of the content process but also see how much work is involved. Also, with these roles clearly laid out it might be easier to lobby for additional web team staff. Here are some example roles for the work flow described earlier to get you started.

Content Requesters

Content Requesters are those members of your organization who suggest additional content, removal, and edits for the website. They work with:

- ▶ Content Creators (arriving at consensus on content message)
- ▶ Content Lead (proposing content)

A work flow issue to consider here is what guidelines are in place for the type of content your Content Requesters can ask for and how those requests will be evaluated. For instance, you might want to make clear that staff can request updates to a page about your summer reading program but that there is a different, overarching process for major content requests that are more like website features rather than simple updates to web copy (such as creating a video archive of library programs).

Content Creators

Content Creators write web copy and produce all the content for the site, including creating multimedia and digital objects (PDFs, videos, and whatever other forms of content the site may incorporate). It is important for your Content Creators to have good writing skills and be knowledgeable about the library's vision, mission, and goals, so assign this role carefully. Content Creators work with:

- ▶ Content Editors (arriving at consensus on edits)

Content Editors

Content Editors are your site's fact checkers and proofreaders. They are the folks who edit your site content in accordance with a pre-established style guide, ensure that the copy is web written, and request updated copy from Content Creators. A skill you are looking for in a good Content Editor is attention to detail. Content Editors work with:

► Content Creators (arriving at consensus on edits)
► Content Approvers (arriving at consensus on edits)

Content Approvers

Content Approvers do the final check and sign-off before content gets published. This role should likely rest with someone who has a level of authority at the library (like someone on the administrative staff or another staff member who is specifically empowered to approve/deny content updates). Content Approvers work with:

► Content Editors (arriving at consensus on edits)
► Content Publishers (delivering ready-to-publish content)

Content Publishers

Content Publishers do just that—press the button to make content go live once it has received the nod from all the other content roles. They are also responsible for updating the content audit when content is published or updated. Content Publishers work with:

► Content Approvers (receiving ready-to-publish content)

A work flow consideration to keep in mind here is how will content be situated before going live? Will it be submitted via e-mail, or will it live in draft status in a content management system? It is important to determine and maintain a standard for how long it will take for content to be published after being approved.

Web Content Leads

Web Content Leads oversee the entire content process, establish the style guide and all other guidelines, and are responsible for auditing and assessing web content on an ongoing basis. Your Web Content Lead should have many of the skills already discussed, such as good web writing skills, copyediting skills, knowledge of the library strategic directions and plans, and authority to set web policy and guidelines. Web Content Leads work with:

► All roles as needed
► Web Team Leads and User Research Team to determine high-level website goals

Keep in mind, as well, that you might want to create more than one work flow for different types of content creation and updates. For instance, updating how much your library charges for making photocopies might not need the same sort of editorial oversight as explaining how a new service works. If you do choose to have more than one work flow, make sure staff understand the differences and the motivation.

►6

MARKETING

- ► **Be a Virtual Branch**
- ► **Don't Forget Traditional Marketing**
- ► **Use Search Engine Optimization**
- ► **Market through Social Media**
- ► **Market a Website Redesign**
- ► **Maintain Transparent Practices**
- ► **Market Internally**

If you've been following library web trends and practices over the past ten years, you probably remember a time when the library website was thought of as nothing more than a marketing tool for the library. If you're still thinking of your website this way, now is the time to shake up that line of thought and start thinking of your website as a *destination* in and of itself. And it's a destination that needs to be marketed, so let's talk about some strategies for how to do that.

►BE A VIRTUAL BRANCH

Recently, more and more library websites are being treated like "virtual branches," with branch managers and other governance and staffing structures in place to support the website the same way that any other branch is supported. Of course, reconceiving of your website in this manner takes a cultural and organizational shift, so you will have to get support from administration to do this, but it is worth trying to make the case for this shift. Treating the library website as a virtual branch will enable you to think about the site as a destination, offering its own unique resources and services, which will in turn allow you to market it accordingly. It is a win–win both for library staff and, more importantly, for library users.

▶ DON'T FORGET TRADITIONAL MARKETING

There is not much that can be said here that hasn't already been said many times in all avenues of library literature: if your library has a tool, service, or resource you would like your users to actually use, you have to market it! When it comes to marketing your library website, never miss an opportunity to put your URL on any/all media your library produces, from bookmarks to handouts to newspaper ads. If you are treating your website as a virtual branch, why not market it as the only 24/7 library branch around? With a memorable URL and clever tagline, the marketing possibilities in traditional media are limitless.

URL Matters

Having a short and pithy URL will make your marketing efforts easier *and* ensure that your users will actually remember your URL when they need it. If your library is just setting up your web domain, or if you are thinking of changing your existing domain, we recommend as short a URL as you can manage. If you're already stuck with a long URL, remember that you can register and market a shorter web address and simply have all traffic automatically redirect to your existing domain. Also, remember to drop the "http://" when you publish your URL on all your marketing vehicles (modern browsers will resolve just fine without typing in the "http://").

▶ USE SEARCH ENGINE OPTIMIZATION

Search engine optimization (called SEO for short) is the practice of improving the visibility and findability of your website by search engines. Because a high percentage of web traffic is conducted through search engines, it is crucial for your website to be findable by search engines and rank high in the list of search engine results (some would say that if your website is not on the first page of Google results, it might as well not exist).

So how do you increase your site's visibility and findability by search engines? SEO is an extensive field with seasoned practitioners, an extensive body of literature, numerous best (and not-so-best) practices, and even its own lingo. We do not claim to be SEO experts, but we do have a short list of recommendations to boost your library's visibility on search engines (if you use a content management system [CMS] such as Drupal, Joomla, or WordPress on your website, the system often takes care of these things for you):

- Use meta tags (<meta>) in the headers of every page on your site. Be sure to put your library's name, location, and any other pertinent info in your meta tags. Think about ways your users will search for your library on search engines and put those keywords in meta tags.
- Make sure every page uses a title tag (<title>).
- Use headers in meaningful ways. It helps to pay attention to header hierarchies (e.g., <h1>, <h2>, etc.) in your markup, because search engine crawlers pay attention to those.
- Keep your URLs simple and human-readable. Even if you don't use a CMS, you should make a concerted effort to keep your URLs as short, simple, and friendly as possible (this will help not only with SEO but also with recall!).
- Search engines also like alt and title tags on your images, so don't forget about those (bonus: these tags also improve the accessibility of your site).
- One of the basic rules of SEO is the more your site is linked on other sites, the more visible it becomes to search engines. There are various ways to accomplish this, one of which is social media integration, which we talk about next.

▶MARKET THROUGH SOCIAL MEDIA

By now, social media should be an integrated part of your library's marketing strategy and your website's content strategy. While tweets and Facebook posts shouldn't be written in marketing speak, they should be purposeful and deliberate. Plan on using your most popular social media channels to promote your library *as well as* your website— remember: it's another destination for access to your resources and services! Once you have established social media channels and made connections with your community members in social media spaces, there is no limit to the ways in which you can use those connections to provide information about your library/website. Social media channels can also be an effective way to recruit people for usability testing and other user research projects.

▶MARKET A WEBSITE REDESIGN

A website redesign project provides a great opportunity to devise a communication and marketing plan for your website. It is tempting to simply assume that any change to your current website will be eagerly embraced by your users as an improvement, and even though that might be the case, it's important to remember that repeat visitors to any website (no matter how good or bad that website is) develop expectations and habits, and flipping the switch on a brand-new website without any prior notice could leave your regular users disoriented at best and downright frustrated at worst. So, as you develop your redesign plan, it's a good idea to develop a communication and marketing plan at the same time. Consider some of the following strategies as you develop this plan:

- ▶ Involve your users and community members in the redesign process as much as possible. If you have a website redesign project team, consider including a couple of community members on the team.
- ▶ Start a blog or webpage devoted to the redesign project. The University of Windsor Library provides a good example with their redesign blog, called *Leddy By Design* (http://infoservices.uwindsor .ca/leddywebdev/), where they chronicle the redesign process and use the blog to engage the community in a discussion about various aspects of web design. Another excellent example is North Carolina State University Library's *Notes from the Redesign Team* (http://news.lib.ncsu.edu/redesign), which details the usability tests conducted, shows the design process, and highlights the personas they developed.
- ▶ Use every usability testing recruitment drive as an opportunity to get the word out that you are working to improve the library website!

Remember that your communication and marketing efforts shouldn't end once you have launched your brand-new website. Instead, use all the marketing channels discussed (traditional media, social media, SEO, etc.) to continue to drive traffic to your site and get your community excited about the redesigned website. You might also think about setting up a table in the library and/or other high-traffic locations in the community to proudly announce the redesigned website and have library staff on hand to show users the site on a laptop, tablet, and/or another mobile device. Also, consider developing a series of screencasts to accompany the redesigned website to orient online users to the new site, paying particular attention to how they can accomplish high-use functions (like renewing a book, finding library hours, etc.) on the new site compared to the old one.

▶ MAINTAIN TRANSPARENT PRACTICES

Being transparent about your web practices does not have to be limited to a specific web project like a redesign. If you constantly communicate with your community about your web practices and plans, you build goodwill and will likely see a higher amount of engagement when, for example, you attempt to recruit participants for usability testing and user research. We mentioned the idea of a redesign blog earlier, as an example of one way to be transparent about a redesign project. You might also consider starting a blog to keep track of *all* of the UX work you do. The *Harvard Library Innovation Laboratory* (http://librarylab.law.harvard.edu/blog/) is an example of such a blog, where the bloggers discuss technology projects underway at the library. Other similar examples are *Ohio State University Library Labs* (http://library.osu.edu/blogs/labs/), Penn Libraries' "labs.library" (https://labs.library.upenn.edu/), and Vanderbilt University Library's *Test Pilot* (http://testpilot.library.vanderbilt.edu/).

You might think that it's unrealistic that many library users will be interested in your development, user research, and design processes, so why bother publishing them? We believe that simply having this information available is valuable both to your user community and to your peer community. Also, if anyone ever has questions or concerns about the website you'll have a resource to show them why the site/resource is the way it is.

▶ MARKET INTERNALLY

One final note about marketing your library website: As important as it is to promote your site as a virtual branch to your user community, it is equally important to market your site *internally* to your colleagues at the library. They can be the best advocates for any web project, from the biggest redesign to the smallest iterative change, so it is important to communicate website changes to them early and often. For example, if you decide to set up a redesign blog to chronicle your redesign project, you can use that blog to communicate with staff as well as users. The blog can demonstrate that decisions about the website haven't been made capriciously and that changes are research based. Therefore, the blog can become a useful tool when talking to staff about the website and can come in handy if anyone suggests arbitrary changes to the site. And, most important, it can get staff on board with website decisions well in advance of making changes, which is the first and most important step to getting them to be advocates for the website!

►7

BEST PRACTICES

- ► Optimize Search Capabilities
- ► Make Navigation Straightforward
- ► Maintain Authenticity
- ► Keep Users Oriented
- ► Have a Mobile Website
- ► Keep the Visual Design Simple
- ► Engage the Community
- ► Write for Clarity

Because there's no such thing as a perfect website, no library website is perfect. Some, however, are better than others, and we can learn from them. Here are some websites that, while not perfect, have outstanding elements.

►OPTIMIZE SEARCH CAPABILITIES

Because searching for library items is the most common thing people do on library websites, the Darien (CT) Public Library website gets top mention. Its catalog and website are tightly integrated. They've done the back-end work, and this relieves patrons of the burden of being exposed to multiple interfaces (see Figure 7.1; http://www.darien library.org/). Another worthwhile example of good search integration is Oakville Public Library (Ontario, Canada), which uses BiblioCommons to provide a seamless website/OPAC searching and browsing experience (see Figure 7.2; http://www.opl.on.ca/).

The Miami University Libraries (Oxford, OH) homepage features multiple search options front and center in a clear, well-integrated layout (see Figure 7.3; http://www.lib.muohio.edu/).

► Figure 7.1: Darien Public Library

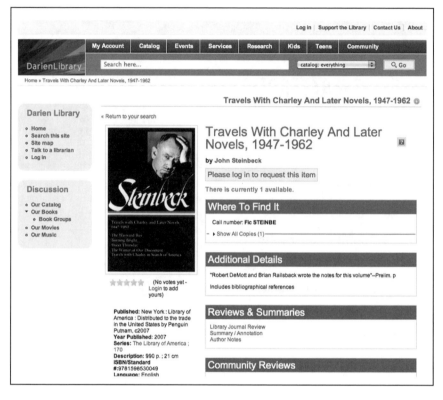

► MAKE NAVIGATION STRAIGHTFORWARD

The Topeka and Shawnee County (KS) Public Library website utilizes a broad navigational structure instead of a deep one. This is reflected in how they present this structure to users. The drop-down mega menu is very effective. What's even better, the information within the menus is logically ordered (see Figure 7.4; http://www.tscpl.org/).

New York Public Library has done a fine job of building a navigation system that is easy to use, uses no library-specific lingo, and provides decent orientation to users even after browsing to deeper levels on the site (see Figure 7.5; http://www.nypl.org/).

► MAINTAIN AUTHENTICITY

Authenticity can't be faked. The Vancouver (BC) Public Library website shows how powerful featuring authentic library users can be.

▶ Figure 7.2: Oakville Public Library

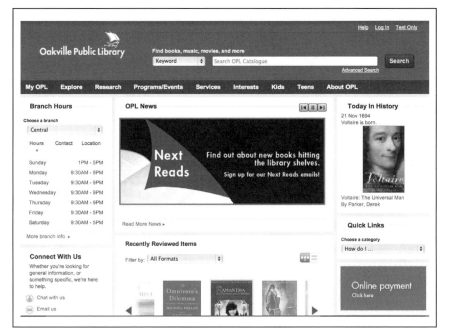

▶ Figure 7.3: Miami University Libraries

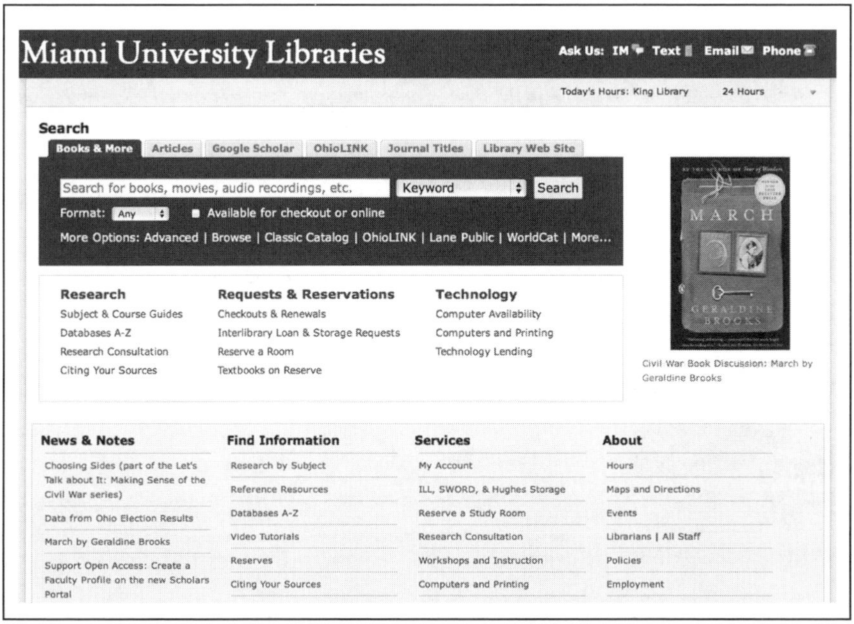

► Figure 7.4: Topeka and Shawnee County Public Library

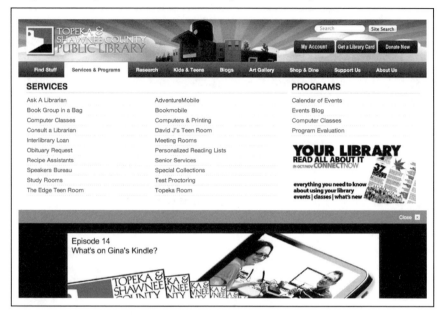

► Figure 7.5: New York Public Library

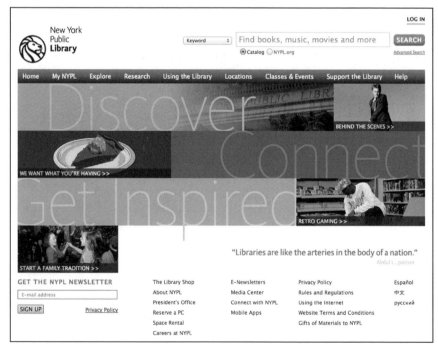

The photographs and blurbs tell people's stories and draw users into the site (see Figure 7.6; http://www.vpl.ca/).

▶KEEP USERS ORIENTED

Each section of the San José Public Library website features a distinct color. This helps orient users and increases a sense of place (see Figure 7.7; http://www.sjpl.org/).

Bridging the web and physical world is a way for libraries to add value to both experiences. The D.H. Hill Library at North Carolina State University does this with its GroupFinder, letting people tell colleagues where in the library they are (see Figure 7.8; http://www.lib.ncsu.edu/groupfinder/).

▶ Figure 7.6: Vancouver Public Library

▶ Figure 7.7: San José Public Library

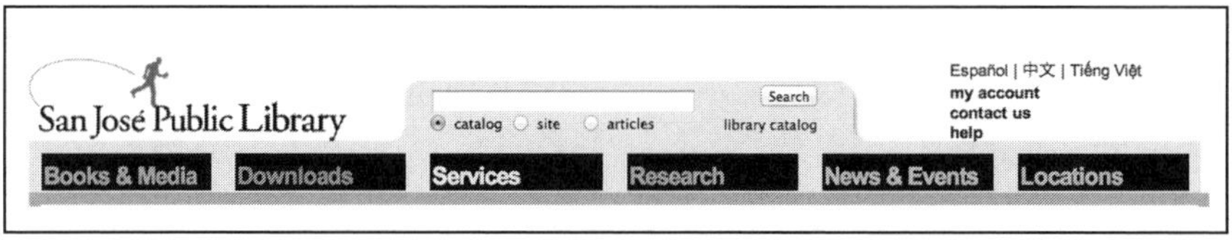

▶ Figure 7.8: D.H. Hill Library at North Carolina State University

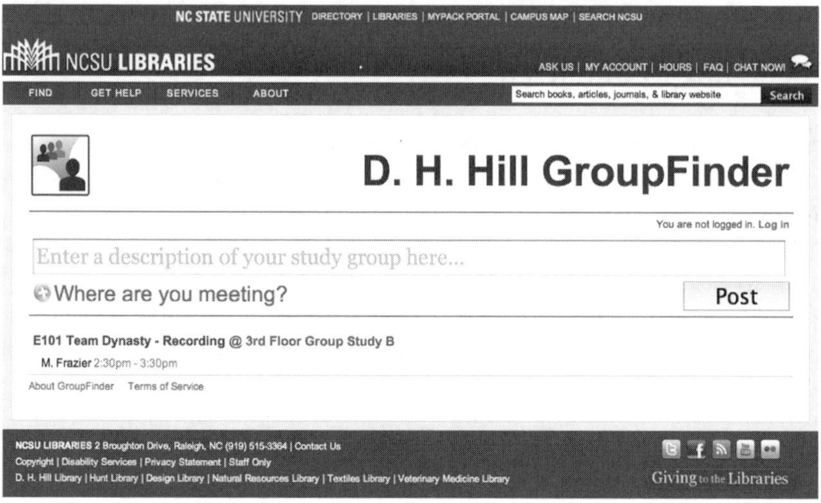

▶ HAVE A MOBILE WEBSITE

The Skokie (IL) Public Library has an extremely functional and attractive mobile website (see Figure 7.9; http://www.skokielibrary .info/mobile/).

▶ Figure 7.9: Skokie Public Library

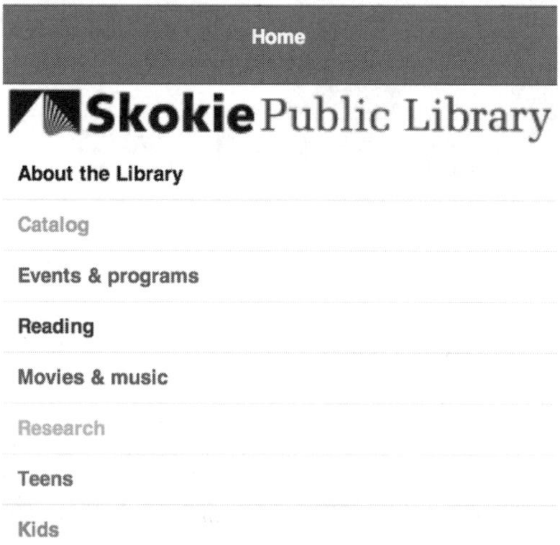

The Ryerson University Library and Archives (Toronto, Canada) mobile website provides just the right kinds of functionality that makes it an excellent example of a thoughtfully designed mobile website. Integrated audio tours and computer availability are two particularly useful features of the site (see Figure 7.10; http://www.ryerson.ca/library/mobile/).

▶ KEEP THE VISUAL DESIGN SIMPLE

The Salt Lake City Public Library website uses vibrant images and bold colors within a minimal design framework, which makes for a delightful user experience (see Figure 7.11; http://www.slcpl.lib.ut.us/).

The Harvard College Library website is a great example of a simple design that uses color and type for maximum impact and ease of use (see Figure 7.12; http://hcl.harvard.edu/).

▶ Figure 7.10: Ryerson University Library and Archives

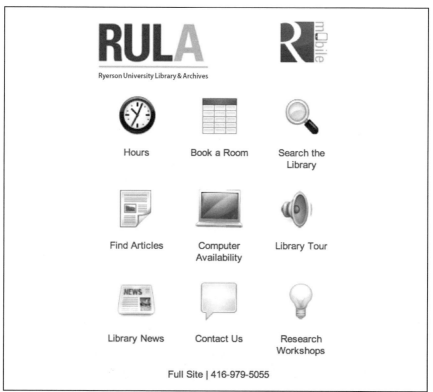

▶ Figure 7.11: Salt Lake City Public Library

▶ Figure 7.12: Harvard College Library

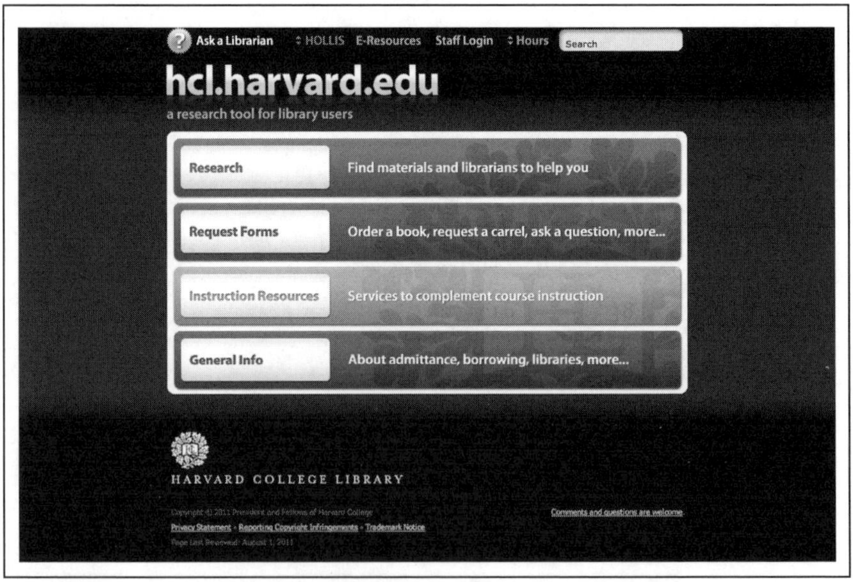

► ENGAGE THE COMMUNITY

The Hennepin County (MN) Library BookSpace accomplishes something not easy to do. It successfully provides a platform for people to connect and share information they've created (see Figure 7.13; http://www.hclib.org/pub/bookspace/).

► WRITE FOR CLARITY

The District of Columbia Public Library uses effective web writing on its Get a Library Card page. Information is chunked and easy to skim (see Figure 7.14; http://dclibrary.org/services/getacard).

► Figure 7.13: Hennepin County Library BookSpace

▶ Figure 7.14: District of Columbia Public Library

▶8

METRICS

- ▶ Use Website Analytics
- ▶ Perform an A/B Test
- ▶ Offer Surveys
- ▶ Perform a Five-Second Test

While recording the number of unique visits to a webpage is simple, measuring someone's experience on a website is notoriously difficult. After all, the fact that visitors looked at a website for two minutes tells you nothing about their reasons for visiting the page or if it met their needs. They could have stayed on the page for those two minutes for a number of reasons: it could have been difficult for them to read, they could have enjoyed every word on the page, or they could have walked away from their computer and forgotten all about it. On top of this is the fact that just because visitors click on a link doesn't mean they read what was on the resulting page. In general, measuring the action on your website can tell you what is happening, but not why.

This might make you want to throw in the towel and forget all about metrics and site analytics, but don't despair. Even though it is impossible to capture all the nuances and the depth of someone's experience with simple numbers, there are still some ways we can collect important data about how our users experience our websites.

▶USE WEBSITE ANALYTICS

Retail websites have an easier time using web analytics than libraries. Because the goal of retail sites is to make money by selling things, they can compare how many site visitors end up becoming customers (this is referred to as the "conversion rate"). There is no discernible conversion rate for library websites, so we often don't have such a straight-forward way to measure success (although it might be worthwhile to try to brainstorm ways to measure success on a library website). What's more, people other than folks in your community might be looking at your website. This is fine, but it muddies the waters because they're not necessarily one of your primary audiences.

What It Is Good For

You can use analytics to see which pages on your website are being looked at and which aren't. This can be useful to make sure patrons are completing whatever it is you've determined are their critical tasks—which is one possible measure of "success." Likewise, you can see if anyone is seeing things that you want them to see. If your analytics report that a relatively small number of users are looking at content that you've deemed important, you can try repositioning it, relabeling it, or increasing the number of access points and links to that content from other pages on the site.

How to Use It

We recommend installing Google Analytics (http://www.google.com/analytics/). It is by far the most popular analytics tool on the web, because it is free, easy to set up, and easy to use, and it provides a wealth of customizable reports.

Google Analytics

Here are some of the things you can track using Google Analytics:

About your content:	**About your website users:**
► How frequently your site is visited	► Where they live
► What the most popular pages are	► What browsers and operating systems they use
► What search terms bring people to your site	► How often they return to your site
	► How many pages they view
	► How they get to your site

► PERFORM AN A/B TEST

With this technique you present randomly selected website visitors with slightly different webpages and track their behavior. For instance, if you are interested in getting more people to look at the library's events calendar, you can set up a test to serve some users your standard page and other users a redesigned page. Looking at the results, it is often possible to see which design leads to more users actually looking at your events calendar.

What It Is Good For

You need to have a goal for A/B testing to be worth your time. It doesn't necessarily have to be a large goal, but you at least need to be curious about how a proposed change will alter users' behavior. In this way, it is useful for assessing the effectiveness of proposed language, labeling, layout, and color changes to a page. For instance, someone might think that changing the word "databases" to "research" might cause more people to find your library's online information resources. A/B testing can answer that question. A/B tests are particularly useful for testing calls to action, such as phrases used to encourage online card sign-ups or donating to the library.

How to Use It

If you're already using Google Analytics, it makes sense to use Google Website Optimizer for A/B testing. With just a bit of JavaScript inserted into your page, you can have an A/B test running with minimal effort. You'll need a fair amount of traffic on the page for the test to have any statistical significance. In some cases you might need to let the test run for a long time.

One final word of advice about A/B testing: when setting up different versions of the same page, it's a good idea to keep the differences to a minimum. For example, page A shouldn't be drastically different from page B, because if they are, it's difficult to actually gauge what the test results are dependent on. Keep the differences between pages to one or two and you will have a better sense of your users' preferences and behaviors and how those preferences and behaviors match your desired outcomes.

▶ OFFER SURVEYS

Surveys work well when you are interested in gauging your users' level of satisfaction with your website and how the site works for them.

What They Are Good For

Surveys can be useful for assessing people's opinions. Of course, people's opinions are sometimes different from how they actually behave, but surveys can still serve as an instructive data point. Consider conducting a short annual survey asking people to rate your site overall, its ease of use, and its ability to help them complete tasks.

How to Use Them

SurveyMonkey (http://www.surveymonkey.com/) is a popular tool for easily and quickly creating online surveys. Our advice: use it sparingly. When implemented as a pop-up on a website, they can be very annoying and disruptive to a user's work flow. As an alternative to the survey pop-up, you might consider putting a link to the survey on your homepage for a certain period of time. Using this method, it will likely take longer for you to gather the amount of data you would like, but maintaining your users' goodwill is worth it!

There are entire textbooks devoted to research methods and good practices to follow when creating surveys, so we'd advise taking a look at some of those practices before drafting your survey questions. Ultimately, the quality of survey data you gather is only as good as the questions you ask! One example of a good practice when drafting survey questions is that when you ask someone to rate your site or a feature on your site, you should use a realistic scale. Providing two choices such as "I completed my task" and "I didn't complete my task" will give you much more meaningful results than if you asked them to rate their experience with a 1–10 scale.

Three Quick Survey Design Tips

1. **Beware survey fatigue:** Web surveys are easy to ignore, and your users will do just that if they are experiencing survey fatigue—that state of irritation caused by being asked to complete multiple online surveys in a short span of time. If you've already surveyed your users in the past few months (even about different topics unrelated to the website), hold off on posting the website survey for a while.

2. **Short and simple is best:** No one likes to fill in pages upon pages of an online survey. Keep your survey to a single, scannable page, and be clear up front about how long it will take to complete the survey (e.g., "This survey will take approximately five minutes to complete.").

3. As Jakob Nielsen says, **divide and conquer:** If you absolutely need to ask a large number of questions, try splitting them up into multiple surveys that are randomly delivered to different survey respondents. Although this means that no one user is responding to every question, it will probably give you a better completion rate because each survey is shorter. (Read more from Nielsen on this topic at http://www.useit.com/alertbox/20040202.html.)

▶ PERFORM A FIVE-SECOND TEST

As the name suggests, a five-second test presents a user with a webpage (or mockup or wireframe) for five seconds and then asks a series of questions about the page. The five-second test is a classic memory game that is intended to test user recall.

What It Is Good For

You wouldn't use a five-second test in place of a classic usability test, but the ability to quickly test user recall is useful in a number of scenarios. Your marketing department will like this type of test, because it is generally considered to be a good way to test brand identity (e.g., did the users notice the logo? What color was it? Will they remember it and associate it with our organization?). In addition, five-second tests can actually provide some good usability metrics for issues such as color or placement of an icon, image, or button. Five-second tests will not delve into the cause of usability problems on your website, but they can be extremely useful if you want to poll a large number of users on a simple question related to preference and recall.

How to Use It

A number of web utilities can provide you with everything you need to conduct five-second tests for your website. We like Clue (http://www.clueapp.com/) and FiveSecondTest (http://fivesecondtest.com/). Clue is a simple memory test that asks users what they remember about the page they have just viewed for five seconds, and FiveSecond Test allows you to provide your own questions to ask the user after the five-second page view is up. While both sites provide a slick way to conduct five-second tests remotely, you can just as easily do five-second tests in person, with paper mockups or wireframes and a pen and paper to scribble down users' responses to your questions.

Remember to keep your test goals and recall questions simple (one or two goals and four questions at the most). You don't want to feel like your design has failed simply because your test goals are too lofty and your questions too complex!

▶9

DEVELOPING TRENDS

▶ **Watch for New Ways to Discover and Access Library Resources**

▶ **Create a Mobile Website**

▶WATCH FOR NEW WAYS TO DISCOVER AND ACCESS LIBRARY RESOURCES

In the introduction to this book we mentioned what we like to call "the catalog problem": the fact that librarians have very little control over the visual design and behavior of the single most important online resource for our patrons. Most of our catalogs are ugly and difficult to use, and there's not much we can do about it.

Is there a solution? In theory, libraries could band together and demand better interfaces and visual design from integrated library system (ILS) vendors. This is unlikely to happen for a number of reasons. First, there doesn't seem to be sufficient concern about this issue to rally the troops and create a movement. Even if libraries were to band together, they have very little leverage in this situation. Libraries could threaten to move from ugly and difficult ILSs to a more desirable option, but there simply aren't outstanding options that make large and complicated migration projects worthwhile.

A promising response to the catalog problem is the development of discovery layer overlays like VuFind, SOPAC, BiblioCommons, Summon, EDS, and others. Discovery layers enable libraries to use the bibliographic data in their ILSs but customize the way that data is displayed. Newer discovery layer products also provide journal content, making the search experience even more seamless as users are able to search website, catalog, and journal article content through a single interface. This seamless experience certainly helps eliminate the mental burden of being presented with multiple interfaces and creates a more cohesive user experience.

There are also multiple open source library ILS projects in development that have all the potential to give libraries more control over their interfaces. This is promising but because these projects require a complete ILS replacement, it is arguably more difficult for many libraries to do. These difficulties have manifested in problematic implementations. For instance, the King County (WA) Library System's implementation of Evergreen (http://catalog.kcls.org/), while fairly attractive, lacked finesse and reliability upon launch.

The catalog problem is mutating. An increasing number of patrons want their books in e-book format, and library e-book offerings are fraught with interaction design and user experience problems. Because library e-books are rarely included in libraries' main catalogs, we're heaping additional navigational and interaction burden on patrons.

► CREATE A MOBILE WEBSITE

Libraries can't ignore the emerging importance of mobile platforms. Some libraries are responding to growth in mobile penetration by developing mobile apps and interfaces for their users. Developing mobile interfaces often requires even more attentiveness to user behaviors, and, because mobile devices and platforms differ so greatly, keeping up with user behaviors can be a challenge. In the most basic terms, mobile interfaces are necessarily stripped of extraneous design elements, because those elements are often too resource intensive. When you're dealing with mobile browsing on small-format screens you don't have the real estate, bandwidth, or time to deal with anything but the essentials. Additionally, mobile functionality (like location awareness) is having a huge impact on the way mobile interfaces are developed.

A related developing trend to keep in mind is the impact mobile browsing is having on the way we develop our regular websites. Increasingly, there is evidence in the usability literature that users are starting to seek out mobile versions of websites even when they are not using mobile devices. The obvious reason for this is that mobile websites tend to be simpler, clearer, and contain only the most essential information required by the majority of users. Some web developers are even going so far as to design for mobile devices first and only then tackling the regular versions of websites. The argument here is that designing for a mobile version of your site will require you to do the difficult work of determining your users' critical tasks and distilling only the necessary content and functionality into that mobile site. Once that work is done, your results can inform the design, functionality, and content decisions you make for your regular website.

The valuable lesson for libraries here is that the mobile experience and changing user expectations will force us to reverse engineer the user experience of our regular websites to be as lightweight, small, and easy to navigate as possible. A noble goal!

RECOMMENDED READING

▶ PRINT RESOURCES

Bowles, Cennydd, and James Box. 2010. *Undercover User Experience Design.* Berkeley, CA: New Riders Press.

> This book provides practical ideas for integrating user experience strategies into situations with limited support and budgets.

Brown, Dan M. 2010. *Communicating Design: Developing Web Site Documentation for Design and Planning.* Berkeley, CA: New Riders Press.

> *Communicating Design* provides a detailed outline and explanation of user experience design deliverables, such as wireframes, site maps, and flowcharts.

Cooper, Allan. 2004. *The Inmates Are Running the Asylum: Why High Tech Products Drive Us Crazy and How to Restore the Sanity.* Sams-Pearson Education.

> This book, mostly about software and product design, is often criticized as being a bit self-congratulatory, but it presents a good case for folding user-centered design into the development process.

Garret, Jesse James. 2010. *The Elements of User Experience: User-Centered Design for the Web and Beyond.* 2nd ed. Berkeley, CA: New Riders Press.

> This should be required reading by anyone keen to understand the principles of user experience design.

Halvorson, Kristina. 2009. *Content Strategy for the Web.* Berkeley, CA: New Riders Press.

> The author makes the case for the importance of website content and will help you develop a plan for creating content that's usable, useful, and desirable.

Krug, Steve. 2005. *Don't Make Me Think: A Common Sense Approach to Web Usability.* 2nd ed. Berkeley, CA: New Riders Press.

> This is an entertaining primer to website usability. Give copies of this book to anyone involved with your website.

Krug, Steve. 2009. *Rocket Surgery Made Easy: The Do-It-Yourself Guide to Finding and Fixing Usability Problems.* Berkeley, CA: New Riders Press.

> Most likely, all you need to know about usability testing for your library is in this book. It is a quick and fun read.

Merholz, Peter, et al., for Adaptive Path. 2009. *Subject to Change: Creating Great Products and Services for an Uncertain World.* Sebastopol, CA: O'Reilly Media.

> From UX heavy hitters at Adaptive Path, this book makes the case for designing experiences rather than products.

Morville, Peter. 2006. *Information Architecture for the World Wide Web.* 3rd ed. Sebastopol, CA: O'Reilly Media.

> Widely considered to be the information architecture Bible, this book covers everything you need to know about building a solid architecture for your website—from IA theory all the way to practical advice for IA/web practitioners.

Mulder, Steve, and Ziv Yaar. 2006. *The User Is Always Right: A Practical Guide to Creating and Using Personas for the Web.* Berkeley, CA: New Riders Press.

> Here is everything you need to know about developing personas and putting them to use for your web development projects.

Muller-Brockmann, Josef. 2007. *Grid Systems in Graphic Design.* 2nd ed. Sulgen, Switzerland: Niggli.

> This classic text from the Swiss typographer illustrates how grids are a useful design tool and how to use them.

Norman, Donald. 2002. *The Design of Everyday Things.* New York: Basic Books.

> First published in 1988 as *The Psychology of Everyday Things*, this is a classic in the field of user experience design. There's nothing about creating websites in this book, but it is worthwhile background reading.

Reddish, Janice. 2007. *Letting Go of the Words: Writing Web.* San Francisco: Morgan Kaufmann.

> This is a must read for anyone contributing content to a website. It contains great examples of writing that is both appropriate and inappropriate for the web as well as many practical tips.

Spencer, Donna. 2009. *Card Sorting.* New York: Rosenfeld Media.

> This book shows you how to use card sorts to better understand how people think about content and categories.

Unger, Russ, and Carolyn Chandler. 2009. *A Project Guide to UX Design: For User Experience Designers in the Field or in the Making.* Berkeley, CA: New Riders Press.

> The authors provide an overview of many aspects of UX, with a slant toward designing for the web.

Vinh, Khoi. 2010. *Ordering Disorder: Grid Principles for Web Design*. Berkeley, CA: New Riders Press.

This book is less practical than theoretical, but it is still informative.

Wroblewski, Luke. 2008. *Web Form Design: Filling in the Blanks*. New York: Rosenfeld Media.

The author provides a practical treatment of webforms and all the interactive elements you need to consider when developing forms for your website.

Young, Indi. 2008. *Mental Models: Aligning Design Strategy with Human Behavior*. New York: Rosenfeld Media.

Mental Models presents a systematic method for determining how people behave and how your organization can meet their needs.

▶WEB RESOURCES

Boxes and Arrows. http://www.boxesandarrows.com/.

This web magazine is devoted to all things design.

A List Apart. http://www.alistapart.com/.

Appropriately subtitled, "For people who make websites," A List Apart is jam-packed with useful articles about web design.

UIE: User Interface Engineering. http://www.uie.com/articles/.

Jared Spool and his associates provide a great collection of articles, podcasts, and other UX resources.

Usability4Lib. http://www.library.rochester.edu/usability4lib.

This electronic discussion list is for usability professionals working in or developing for libraries.

Useit.com. http://www.useit.com/.

Here you will find a collection of articles, reports, and news by Jakob Nielsen, one of the preeminent usability experts.

UX Booth. http://www.uxbooth.com/.

UX Booth is an active UX community blog.

UX Magazine. http://www.uxmag.com/.

This collection of articles devoted to UX design is regularly updated.

UX Zeitgeist. http://rosenfeldmedia.com/uxzeitgeist/.

This continually updated collection of user experience books is curated by the user experience design community.

INDEX

Page numbers followed by the letter "f" indicate figures.

ABOUT THE AUTHORS

Aaron Schmidt, in the past eight years, has been a circulation clerk, reference librarian, and library director. Shortly after completing his MLIS at Dominican University, Schmidt saw the potential of applying new media technology to libraries and launched successful programs at his suburban Chicago public library. Helping the library connect to its community through things such as instant messaging, weblogs, and social software led to Aaron publishing articles in *Library Journal, School Library Journal, Library High Tech News, Online,* and others. He has presented on the topic of library technology and usability throughout the United States and in Canada, the United Kingdom, the Netherlands, and Spain. In 2005, Schmidt was named a *Library Journal* Mover & Shaker.

Schmidt moved to Portland, Oregon, in 2006 and became the director of a nearby public library. He helped the library grow and gain full membership in the Washington County Cooperative. During this time he continued to write, give presentations and workshops, and work for other libraries as a consultant.

Next he acted as the Digital Initiatives Librarian for the District of Columbia Public Library, working from Portland. He helped plan forward-thinking projects for the library, helping them connect to the community and teaching them about the Read/Write Web. He also assisted with website visioning, conducted usability testing, and formed the library's Library 2.0 Interest Group and the library's digital research and development project called DC Library Labs. He created user interfaces for home-brewed self-check machines and iPad-based neighborhood library dashboards. He was part of the team that created the first iPhone and BlackBerry online catalog searching applications.

Currently he is a principal at INFLUX Library Users Experience Consulting and maintains a library and website usability weblog, walkingpaper.org, and can be reached at librarian@gmail.com

Amanda Etches is the Head of Discovery & Access at the University of Guelph Library, where she spends her time guiding teams and projects that are all about making the overall library experience better for users, both in-person and online. Prior to her current role, Amanda was the User Experience Librarian at McMaster University Library.

Amanda is also part of Influx, a user experience consultancy that works with libraries. She has an MA in English Literature and an MISt in Library and Information Science, both from the University of Toronto.

Amanda's research interests include human–computer interaction, information architecture, and web/interaction/UX/service design, and she frequently writes and presents on web design, usability, and user experience practices and trends. Amanda tweets @etches and blogs intermittently at http://e.tches.ca, two places where you are likely to find her feeling guilty about having so much fun doing exactly what she is supposed to be doing. She can also be reached at etchesjohnson@gmail.com.